Common Sense

For the Twenty-First Century

Common Sense

⇛ *for* ⇚

The Twenty-First Century

Blase Bonpane

Radio commentaries and interviews directed
to the formation of an international peace system

Red Hen Press *Los Angeles 2004*

Common Sense for the Twenty-First Century

Cover photomontage by Hugh Stegman 2003

"Peace Flag" created by Peter Dudar and Sally Marr

Book and cover design by Mark E. Cull
Book layout by James Harmon

ISBN 978-1-888996-56-2
Library of Congress Catalog Card Number 2004091978

Second Printing, 2010

The City of Los Angeles Department of Cultural Affairs,
California Arts Council, and
the Los Angeles County Arts Commission
partially support Red Hen Press

First Edition

Red Hen Press
w w w . r e d h e n . o r g

Contents

World Focus Interviews

Introduction

The George W. Bush Years have been the greatest threat to international justice and peace in world history. He has endangered the people of the United States and the world with a vision of endless wars. He has enraged the international community with his banal arrogance and threats. A sycophant media and a constantly clapping Congress revel as cheering sections for his nationalistic fundamentalism and fanatical *jingoism*.

He presides over the dead of Afghanistan, the dead of Iraq, the dead of our loyal troops and wounded without number. Indeed the wounds of his militarism have damaged the people of the planet and called into question the future of the United States of America. George W. Bush came to power under the cloud of non-election. Action taken by the Supreme Court to select him as President has been questioned by leading legal scholars. The Bush presidency recalls the years of the selected President Rutherford Hayes who, as Bush, failed to win the popular vote and who did as much as possible to destroy the period of reconstruction after the Civil War. For four years, Hayes was known as "Your Fraudulency." These commentaries are presented as a judgment on the Bush presidency. Our hope is that the resilient people of the United States will be able to overcome a regime that has done nothing for the common good of the people of the United States and which has endangered the planet on behalf of its military, industrial, gun and prison cronies. The manipulation of fear by war-mongering profiteers is the lowest form of corrupt politics.

Over ninety years ago, January 16, 1914, a college freshman gave a speech *The Call of Our Age* at the Dr. Albert Edwin Smith's Annual Oratorical Contest at Ohio Northern University. He won the $50.00 prize for the best oration. That freshman, an immigrant from Italy who worked his way through school as a printer, was my father, Blase A. Bonpane, a Judge of the Superior Court of Los Angeles County.

 In his entire career, not one of his decisions was ever reversed by a higher court. Written prior to the League of Nations and the United Nations, his oration foretold the necessity of such agencies of international law. As a twenty-year old student at the outset of World War I, my father saw clearly what needed to be done; we had to abolish the war system and to build a peace system. He gave *The Call of Our Age*. The Office of the Americas is responding to his call.

Thanks Dad.

Here is his oration:

Through the silent, solemn, march of the centuries, fraught with strife and struggle, the world has ever gone forward and upward. Entombed in the ages gone by are the shattered remains of tyranny, of iniquity, of human oppression. Lawlessness and brute force are no more the ruling powers. Despotism and unfounded persecution have submitted to law and government. Today we look back from our pinnacle of civilization with surprise and horror to behold "man's inhumanity to man." In all of the civilized world of this era our institutions are for justice and equality. Education smiles with vigor. Christianity sings her song of hope. More than ever before, the world throbs with humanity; more than ever before human suffering is sought to be reduced; more than ever before, the cry of peace and good will resounds throughout the earth.

But alas! In our age of civilization, the vitals of human progress are being forever stunned and sapped of their lifeblood by a dreadful relic of primeval years—that pestilent scourge of war. The fruit of man's handiwork representing years of tireless toil is squandered in a single encounter. The richest in health and vigor, the most promising industrial productiveness, are being drawn from the ranks of youth to quench the bloody thirst of war.

Yet this war has in great part been caused by the unsound reasoning of modern statesmanship. For years the mind of man was misled by that fallacious doctrine that preparation for war secures peace. "Burden the people with taxes, build artificial volcanoes, parade them up and down the high seas and defy the world to attack us!" Then, they said, "We shall have peace." Have we eyes and yet see not that while this policy was being upheld, each nation regarded with jealous eyes any increase in armament by the other? One day England built mammoth war machines; the next day Germany took fright and built more brutal instruments of war; then England, with her horrid and floating earthquakes, was compelled to outclass Germany. And so it went, until the heavy burden of taxation blighted and blistered the lives of the people. In the tremendous conflict abroad, even the dullest should see the fallacy of armed peace. Every new battleship, every new gun represented a thought of war and these thoughts piled mountain high contributed to the present calamity. And think of the result! Think of the flower of manhood which has been swept away; think of the Kaiser's devastating march toward Paris; of the German's charge in the siege of Liege where the Teutons pressed up to the cannon's mouth and melted away; of the beautiful Antwerp, once rich with life and happiness, torn to pieces by the merciless machines of war. Belgium once beamed with happiness. Today the country is a waste, with cities and towns destroyed, fields and factories ruined and its roads filled with homeless wanderers. This, then, is the work of armament; the work of armed peace! Thus upon the brazen brow of Europe's martial grandeur is stamped the bold statement that, "Who undertakes by the sword, shall fall by the sword."

Still worse than war's present devastation is its terrible curse upon future generations. And what of those that survive the cataclysm of war? Civilization and Christianity suffer in their hands. For the first time, it gives to the great masses the taste of the bullet, the sword, the bayonet. It brings them in personal contact with rapine and plunder. Murder, arson, theft are but trifling crimes to men who have been taught that all things are fair in war. Tender feelings will be blunted, sympathies stilled and consciences hushed. Men who left their homes whole hearted, kind and gentle will return from war with the stain of blood upon their hands and the spirit of vengeance in their hearts. It is this that stuns humanity abroad, that nourishes murder, that promotes anarchy when people find that governments not only destroy the lives of father and son, not only impoverish the family for no fault of its own, but also place the heavy burden of oppressive taxes upon unwilling sufferers from needless wars. Yes, "Wars are not paid for in war time," says Benjamin Franklin, "the bill comes later."

Oh, the let us have peace for humanity's sake! This is an age of order, not of crime; of morality, not of vice; of life, not of death. Pride, power, influence, the lust for gain—all count nothing today, compared with the lifting of men to a higher and nobler plane; compared with their rescue from the base and ignoble passions which maddening war creates. True, armed conflicts have been glorified in history, but today, as the poet tells us, "the thoughts of men are widened" and our social, our moral, and all our virtuous instincts tell us it is wrong.

Among other virtues, International faith is bound to assume a place. We have seen the Magna Carta of a great federation. It is the Treaty of the Hague. Its spirit shall win. At the second Hague Conference called in the spring of 1907, after a vivid discussion of delicate international questions, it was determined without dissention that: peace is the normal and war the abnormal condition for civilized nations; that relations of sovereign states are properly based upon the principles of justice; that differences between nations should be settled by judicial methods and not by force of war. True, the Hague Court has not been altogether successful. But let us not forget that this tribunal is only a herald of the great power that is yet to be, although even as it is, close to three hundred disputes have been settled by this method. The enforcement of judgments is the defective part of the Hague Court. Vest in it the power to determine controversies; vest in it the power to punish transgressors; vest in it the power to enforce its laws, and the culmination of the process, as with all governmental units, must be the creation of a world executive.

Public opinion has enacted a law against murder; so should international public opinion demand a law against war, which is merely organized murder. Shall we execute a man for taking a single life and glorify nations for slaughtering its thousands? To curb crime, to protect justice, police powers are instituted in all realms. Why not go beyond the transitory interest of a nation and establish an international police power? Just as social deprivation restrains the criminal's passions, so can finances thwarted, subdue nations to obeisance. Let the representatives of the world powers meet in one body! Let a world code be compiled! Let fines be imposed and commerce hindered when nations wrong and offend!

In England is Parliament; in America is Congress where representatives from various parts of the nation meet to act for the public welfare. The component states of these countries each share rights different in some degree from the other. Yet, binding them all together, is an indissoluble tie—the National Government. Consider the development of this spirit among nations! When individual parts of a country can be so bound by a single representative body, what will hinder nations from creating a common assembly with fixed sessions to establish laws of international import? When the rights of these distinctive states can be held inviolate by a Congress or a Parliament what will keep a world power from exerting a like dominion over nations?

Throughout the United States are national guards to maintain law and order. Why not provide international guards to demand the implicit adherence of all countries to this supreme world tribunal? Let them swear allegiance this world code! Let them treat all violations as rebellious! To supplement the federal guards, and to enforce the maritime law, let a navy patrol the high seas, controlled by the Congress of the Nations. Thus impregnable and complete is the shield of law against the din of war with its flaming swords, its dreadful agonies, its racking tortures and ghastly spasms.

A visionary dream, think you? God made humanity one. But man is now divided against himself. The fulcrum of truth and knowledge is becoming higher. Through common interest, through common needs, the world must move towards the unity of all its peoples. America with her heterogeneous population will be a model for the great world power. Public opinion is one mighty force for revolutionizing any institution. With its protection men, will either crush each other in selfish hatred or come together in bonds of respect and sympathy. The generation that fought the Civil War nurtured that spirit since childhood. Southern children were taught that the "black abolitionist" encroached upon Southern rights and fostered slave insurrections. Likewise, Northern children learned to despise Southern slaveholders. And so it is today. Dr. Faunce, President of Brown University, in a recent address said, "Academic influence and training is responsible for the present European war. The teaching in the schools and universities of Europe of the spirit of militarism for the past forty years, today produces the murderous trenches and fields of carnage."

With this in view, what is the duty of the present hour? What is the duty of our age? In our homes, in our schools, in our churches and everywhere, it is our duty to make the coming generation see that peace is grander than war; that to live for a great purpose is nobler than to die; that the development of society is more poetic than flowing blood and frenzied patriotism. Let love for humanity and not for haughty feats of arms be our subjects for popular narratives! Let the mighty pen blaze out the path and make clear the way up which all nations of the earth must come! Let internationalism be our watchword, our aim, our duty. Let us hear the call of our age! Then the golden 'cestus of peace' shall clothe all with celestial beauty; and serene, resplendent, on the summit of human achievement shall stand the miraculous spectacle, the Congress of Nations, with a common purpose of agreeing, not upon military plans, not to foster cruelty and incite other people to carnage, not to bow before the god of battles, but to announce the simple doctrine of peace and brotherhood—our only hope, our only reliance against which all powers of the earth shall not prevail.

January 16, 1914
Ohio Northern University, Ada, Ohio.

xvii

Common Sense

For the Twenty-First Century

Pacifica

Radio Commentaries

KPFK 90.7 FM

Los Angeles, California

November 6, 2001 to April 8, 2004

Hello, this is Blase Bonpane with a comment . . .

War Against Terror
November 6, 2001

What is happening in Afghanistan today?

According to the *New York Times*, there are seven to eight million people in Afghanistan on the verge of starvation. Now, that was before September 11.

Then on September 16 the *New York Times* reported that the United States demanded from Pakistan the elimination of truck convoys that provide much of the food for Afghanistan's civilian population. This was an effort to impose massive starvation on millions of people.

The World Food Program of the United Nations was able to resume aid in early October but distribution was hampered for lack of workers within Afghanistan. Aid agencies began to oppose U.S. airdrops of food as probably doing more harm than good. Doctors Without Borders said that their aid was being hampered by the U.S. bombing. There was also concern of U.S. food drops landing in areas covered with millions of land mines. Now, the *New York Times* reports that just before the harsh winter, 7.5 million Afghanis are in acute need of food. Simultaneous with this report Mr. Bush refused any offer of negotiations.

On the same day, the Special Rapporteur of the United Nations in charge of food pleaded with the U.S. to stop the bombing to prevent millions of victims from starving. This plea was joined by Oxfam and other aid agencies.

We can expect the death of millions within a few weeks as winter moves into Afghanistan. Some twenty years ago, the Reagan administration began declaring that the war against international terrorism would be the core of our foreign policy.

One case is best documented because the judgments of the International Court of Justice, the World Court and the United Nations Security Council. It is a case of terrorism that was even more extreme than the events of September 11. It was the Reagan/U.S. war against Nicaragua which left some 40,000 dead and a country in ruins.

Nicaragua responded, not by terrorism, but by taking the case to the World Court. They had no problem putting together the evidence. The World Court accepted the case of Nicaragua vs. United States and ruled in favor of Nicaragua. The Court identified the unlawful use of force (which is another word for terrorism) by the U.S. and ordered the U.S. to terminate the crime and pay reparations of some 17 billion dollars. The U.S. dismissed the Court's judgment and thereby disempowerd the court by not accepting its jurisdiction.

Then Nicaragua went to the Security Council with a resolution asking that all states observe international law. The United States vetoed the resolution. Now we stand as the only nation on record to be condemned by the World Court for international terrorism and for vetoing a Security Council resolution to observe international law.

Nicaragua then went to the General Assembly with a similar resolution regarding international law. The United States, Israel and El Salvador voted against the resolution. The following year there were only two votes against the observation of international law: the U.S. and Israel.

The response of the U.S. to the World Court and Security Council was to escalate the war in Nicaragua. The terrorist army of mercenaries was ordered to attack soft targets and keep away from the Nicaraguan army. They attacked agricultural collectives, health clinics and civilian communities with the help of the most modern communications equipment.

Time magazine cheered the victory of the Contras by saying the success of these methods ". . . to wreck the economy and prosecute a long and deadly war until the exhausted natives overthrow the unwanted government themselves" with a cost to us that us that is minimal and leaving the victims with wrecked bridges, sabotaged power stations and ruined farms.

Indeed, terrorism works. Terrorism is not the weapon of the weak. Nazi terror claimed it was protecting local populations from terror. We began using these methods under the title of "low intensity warfare." The very thought that Nicaragua might have the right to defend itself was considered outrageous. Just think, they rumored that Nicaragua was getting MIG jets from USSR. They were breaking the rule that we were the only nation that could sell jet fighters to Latin America.

These MIGs were said to be a threat to the U.S. According to Reagan, Nicaragua was only a two-day march from Harlingen, Texas. The U.S. actually declared a national emergency in 1985 to protect us from the threat of Nicaragua. The idea that Nicaragua had the right to defend its airspace against a superpower attack that was directing terrorist forces to attack undefended civilian targets was considered outrageous.

Then there was the appointment of John Negroponte, the local supervisor of the terrorist war in Nicaragua from the base in Honduras, for which the U.S. was condemned. And now he is the Ambassador to the United Nations. Now Nicaragua is the second poorest country in the hemisphere. And the threats continued through the 80s and 90s. Today, Nicaragua has just lost another election after many threats of our recent delegation. State terror was even more extreme in El Salvador and Guatemala.

The worst violator of human rights in the 90s and in this new century is Colombia. In 1999, Colombia replaced Turkey as the leading recipient of arms from the United States.

From 1984 to 1999, tens of thousands were killed; 3,500 towns and villages were destroyed and 80% of the arms came from the U.S. But Turkish terror was called counter-terror. Turkey will now join the Coalition Against Terror? The same F-16s used by Turkey to bomb its own people were used to assist in the war against Serbia. Resistance is called terror.

Algeria, one of the most terrorist-ridden states, welcomes the U.S. war on terror. Russia wants the U.S. to support its war with Chechnya and is supporting our position. China wants us to support its battles against Muslim separatists in Western China.

The Search for Osama Bin Ladin

November 15, 2001

It seems to me that we should look at the world in terms of what would be best for our children and all children. Here comes the Northern Alliance which used to be the Soviet side and which was the side we attacked when Osama Bin Laden was fighting for us.

The Afghani women we have heard from remind us that the Northern Alliance was in charge of their country from 1992 to 1996. They are considered to be rapists and looters. These Afghani women state that the Northern Alliance will simply intensify ethnic and religious conflicts and will fan the fires of an endless civil war. They give the example of the recent massacres that took place in Mazar-e-Sharif. These women are appealing to the United Nations and to the world to send in an effective peace keeping force before the Northern Alliance can repeat their crimes of 1992-1996.

We will never attempt to justify what took place in New York City and Washington on September 11, 2001. And we must never attempt to justify the bombing of Afghanistan either. The end does not justify the means. And apparently, there is no end.

Any deficient leadership can start a war. But that same leadership can rarely stop a war. Allegedly, we went to war to find someone who was living in Afghanistan. After a rain of 15,000 pound bombs, fuel air bombs and cluster bombs, it would seem difficult to identify our suspect either dead or alive.

Just think about the means used to give this victory to the dubious leadership of the Northern Alliance. Under a cloak of secrecy we used weapons of mass destruction. Untold numbers of innocent civilians have been slaughtered. There is a history of this searching for one man and slaughtering many. On Christmas of 1989 we were searching for Manuel Norriega in Panama. In that search, Stealth Bombers blew away the neighborhoods of El Chorillo and San Miguelito in Panama City. But we got our man who is now languishing in a federal prison. Then there was

8

the search for Saddam Hussein. 500,000 troops went looking for him, bombs have been falling on Iraq for over ten years, an embargo has led to some 5,000 Iraqi children dying every month. And Saddam is just fine, thank you. He eats well and remains free. And now the search for Osama can go on for ever. It has become kind of a "Where's Waldo" situation. Maybe he is in Iraq; let's do more bombing over there, maybe he's in Syria, let's bomb over there.

And what does this do to the spiritual and physical environment of the world? The world military at peace is the biggest threat to the spiritual and physical environment because of its ideology of might makes right. The physical toxicity of the military has become obvious in the United States where no superfund is large enough to clean up the nuclear waste.

Well if the military at peace is the biggest single threat to the environment, what about the military at war? The military at war is planetary suicide. The planet cannot be sustained with the military at war. Nuclear weapons are planet busters. They will make our beautiful planet look like the Moon, like Pluto or Mars. There will be simply not be anyone left at home.

Here is a case where our purported victory in Afghanistan might be used foster new and uglier wars as well as perpetuate the Israeli-Palestinian conflict.

It appears to be a *Phyrric* victory.

A Fantasy Visit to the
Oval Office for Christmas

Decembr 6, 2001

Another restless night. I am in the oval office having the following con-
versation:

"Hello, Mr. President, I want to thank you for the opportunity to present another perspective on your current policy. I do hope you will share
these thoughts with your advisers.

"An international crime against humanity was committed against the
United States and some sixty other countries by virtue of the attacks on
September 11, 2001. The United States had to respond. We believe,
however, that it was a mistake to call this heinous act a war. The perpe-
trators of this crime were from Saudi Arabia and Egypt. Our attack was
on Afghanistan with the allegation that the terrorist leader was based in
that country. We are pleased with the demise of the Taliban regime. But
ethically, we do not believe that the "end justifies the means."

"The Wazir Akbarhan hospital in Kabul was bombed and 13 women
were killed in the Gynecology Department. Two-hundred people were
killed in the hospital at Herat. Red Cross facilities have been bombed
twice. A center for the destruction of land mines was destroyed. Cluster
bombs, which are prohibited by international law and whose bomblets
are the same yellow color as food packets, have killed countless civilians
as have 15,000-pound bombs. AC-130 planes were filled with 70,000
pounds of ammunition and fired huge gatling guns on populations. These
weapons can put a bullet in every square foot of a football field as they
fly by. The community of Kama Ado has been eliminated from the face
of the earth.

"During evening prayer time, the village of Karam was struck killing
a substantial number of the inhabitants. 2,000 pound bombs fell on the
Qila Meer Abas neighborhood two miles south of Kabul airport. A 2,000
pound bomb hit the Red Crescent Clinic.

"Our new allies referred to as the Northern Alliance are said to be the
key source of the international opium supply. Their product will certainly

10

not help our people. After a costly 'victory' over the Romans, Phyrrus declared that another similar "victory" would ruin him. I think that another victory after Afghanistan will ruin us in the sight of the world. We too are facing a *Phyrric* Victory.

"Some of our own troops have been killed by these bombs together with innocent men women and children who also had no role whatsoever in any attack on the United States.

"The whole world knows that Afghanistan is one of the weakest nations on the planet. What is the message when the strongest attacks the weakest? And now, in the wake of our military attack, millions of Afghans are facing death by starvation.

"We were pleased with the United Nations meeting in Germany to structure a new administration in Afghanistan. But the United Nations should have been empowered in the first place to seek the help of 189 countries to apprehend the criminals of 9/11. A truly international anti-terrorist coalition could have been formed.

"Some advisers are now urging you to attack Iraq. This, of course would mean the end of the limited coalition supporting the Afgahnistan war. International outrage would follow. We hear of possible attacks on the Sudan, Somalia, Syria, Indonesia, the Philippines and elsewhere. Such attacks will be like gasoline added to a fire.

"It is time for us to declare our interdependence and to utilize all the mechanisms of international law. We can fully implement the International Criminal Court, end land mines throughout the world, end the nuclear menace to our lives, end bacteriological and chemical warfare and all weapons of mass destruction. Substantive disarmament is never a matter of unilateral action. On the contrary, we now have the technology necessary for implementing multilateral international disarmament.

"War making becomes mindless slaughter. Peacemaking requires thought, concern and planetary vision. Will you help us obtain a peaceful solution before the planet is destroyed by the war system? Peace on earth *is* possible.

Thank you for your attention, Mr. President."

State of the Union

January 30, 2002

Since its inception, the Organization of American States has been manipulated by its most powerful member, the United States. Our country has had a vendetta against Haiti and its President Jean Bertrand Aristide. Why? Because of his enormous popularity with the poorest members of that society and his audacity to abolish the Haitian Army. The armies of Latin America have been enforcers of U.S. policies for well over a century. How can these policies be maintained without a Haitian Army?

Isn't it more than curious that the U.S. continued to give aid to Haiti during the dictatorships of Papa Doc Duvalier and Baby Doc Duvalier but continues its attacks of destabilization and disinformation against the most popular and democratic government in the history of Haiti? Desperately needed loans from the Inter-American Development Bank have been blocked by Washington. Unbelievably, Haiti is forced to pay interest on loans which it has not received.

Please call your Representative and ask him/her to end economic sanctions and restore all aid to Haiti. Also Haiti must be forgiven interest on aid it has not received. Capitol Switchboard is 202/224-3121.

Yes, we heard the State of the Union Address. Our summary:

1. The promise of an endless war.

2. An atmosphere of hysteria.

3. The use of our resources to build an ever-greater military machine.

4. Direct threats to at least a dozen nations.

5. A militarized State with impaired civil liberties.

12

6.   Direct threats to the twenty million non-citizens who live in the
      United States

7.   Failure to meet the real needs of the United States including the
      ongoing embarrassment of the world's richest country unable
      to deliver adequate health care, schooling and housing for its
      people.

All of this by the man who said, "You are either with us or with the terror-ists." Just think: "No, we are not with you Mr. Bush, and we are not with terrorists either. We remember our terrorism in the Vietnam War and so do the families of three million people who were killed there. We remember the terrorism of the Contra War and so do the families of 40,000 Nicara-guans who were killed there by an international crime against humanity known as the Iran/Contra scandal. We remember the terrorism of the wars we supported in Guatemala and El Salvador leading to hundreds of thousands of deaths because of our ignorant and shortsighted policies. We remember the terror of the Stealth bombers in Panama in 1989 and the sheer insanity of our attack on Grenada in 1983. We remember the ter-rorist slaughter in Iraq in 1991 and the continuing terror of bombing that country for the past eleven years together with a death-dealing embargo, which is killing thousands of Iraqis every month. We even remember the massacres in Afghanistan as reports of entirely destroyed communities leak out of the absolute censorship of this unnecessary war."
     And we are told that the people we are killing are evil. The ignorance and malice reflected in such statements cries to heaven. We believe that the people of the United States are victims of reckless endangerment by virtue of a war mongering, incompetent and unelected administration. We have paid heavily with our tax money for benefits to the common good of the people of the United States. That money has been squandered on gasoline that is being poured on fires all over the world. We are in extreme danger because of this ignorant and malicious policy.
     In the midst of an endless flow of jingo, the corporate/state-controlled media permits no dissent. We are inspired, however, and eternally grate-ful to the hundreds of people including many Office of the Americas volunteers who participated in bringing the Pacifica Network back to its Mission of being a voice for the voiceless, a voice for justice and peace.

Mutiny

March 15, 2002

The history of mutiny is a history of consciousness. The study of mutiny is far more instructive than the study of imperial victories. But history is written by the victors, so students suffer from the boredom of unrestrained triumphalism.

Mutiny in the Civil War was massive on both sides. Yankee immigrants who did not have $300 to buy their way out of the draft were resentful. Many left their ranks to seek meaningful employment. Mutiny was massive in World War I. General Pershing ordered his officers to execute deserters. Pershing's officers did not comply. General Eisenhower approved the desertion execution of Private Slovick in World War II.

Mutiny is punished by death in absolutist structures. It is simply the doctrine of infallibility as applied to the state. The mutinous and deserters of the Korean War may still be found in various parts of Asia.

The mutiny in Vietnam was an indelible rejection of United States policy. Orders were ignored, officers were assassinated by their own troops. A mutation had taken place in the concept of a soldier as a robot. Soldiers became conscious of how they were being used.

Why have we deprived students of the history of mutiny? It seems we are afraid they too might break from absolutist obedience to tyranny. Mutiny is a substantive component of world history. It must not be ignored. A sharp example of it took place before the Civil War. It was the mutiny of the San Patricio Battalion in the 1846 War with Mexico. The war was a vicious conquest of Mexico, not by Spain, but by the United States. Abe Lincoln opposed the war with Mexico saying that our troops were killed on Mexican soil as "aggressors." Ulysses S. Grant described the war with Mexico as, "The most unjust ever waged by a stronger against a weaker nation." Robert E. Lee expressed similar sentiments.

President Polk was full of fundamentalist manifest destiny and dreamt about taking everything down to Mexico City. The war ended in 1848 with the United States generously taking only half of Mexico.

The Irish immigrants who fled the potato famine in their country came to the United States and were quickly inducted into the United States Army to vanquish Mexico. But United States Captain John Riley, formerly of County Galway, analyzed the situation and determined that this was a war of aggression against the Mexican people. He saw in the Mexicans the same love, the same hospitality and the same Church he had left in Ireland. Why should he fight these beautiful people? He brought his battalion to the Mexican side and fought against the invading gringos. Mexico honors the San Patricio Battalion every year. Ireland honors the San Patricio Battalion every year. We too will honor them once we prefer critical thinking to absolutist conformity.

The history of mutiny is the history of consciousness. Filmmaker Mark Day has directed and produced a superb documentary (The San Patricios) on the San Patricios and revealed the history of a few brave men who abandoned a conquering army to follow their consciences.

Mutiny is not a tragedy. The tragedy is that we feed our young people an endless diet of triumphal material and allow them to be deprived of a truth that hurts and liberates.

Let's take a look at what some Israeli soldiers who will no longer serve have stated and signed in recent weeks:

- We, who understand now that the price of occupation is the loss of the Israel Defense Forces human character and the corruption of the entire Israeli society;

- We who know that the territories are not Israel, and that all settlements are bound to be evacuated in the end;

- We hereby declare that we shall not continue to fight this War of the Settlements. We shall not continue to fight beyond the 1967 borders in order to dominate, expel, starve and humiliate an entire people.

15

Security Council Resolution 1402

April 15, 2002

A football game is a poor analogy for international conflicts. In the ball game there is a level playing field and you root for your team.

In the violence of armed conflicts, however, there is no level playing field and there is no reason to root for the more violent oppressor.

Our commercial media has referred to recent demonstrations as pro-Palestinian or pro-Israel. Here is the useless football analogy.

If the demonstrations are pro-Palestinian, why are so many Jews present? And why are so many Jews protesting in front of Israeli consulates?

The reason is simple. Mature people want to root for justice; they do not want to be a cheering section for their state as some form of idol worship.

No matter how strong the rhetoric, the whole world can see that one side has tanks, one side has military bulldozers, one side has planes, bombs and heavy artillery, one side has helicopters, one side has received hundreds of billions of our tax payers' money.

Now to associate the quest for justice with anti-Semitism is an affront to millions of Jewish people who are demanding justice from their government and to Jewish people who are marching into Palestine with food and medicine.

Everyone knows who the oppressor is and who are the oppressed. Oppressed people will fight back, saying, "Give me liberty or give me death." Yes, profound humiliation and disrespect can actually lead peaceful people to become suicide bombers.

> "Those who make non-violent change impossible make violent change inevitable."
> —John F. Kennedy.

On Saturday, March 30, 2002, Security Council Resolution 1402 was approved calling for the withdrawal of Israeli troops from Palestinian cities. The Security Council reaffirmed previous resolutions and expressed its grave concern at the further deteriorating situation including the suicide bombings in Israel as well as the attacks on the president of the Palestinian Authority. This new resolution calls upon both parties for an immediate ceasefire.

And now, the fifteen-member Security Council of the United Nations, including the United States, holds an emergency meeting insisting on immediate implementation of resolutions demanding an Israeli-Palestinian ceasefire and an Israeli withdrawal from Palestinian cities without delay. Stating that Israel's continued military action against Palestinians is both unacceptable and a violation of international humanitarian law. This decision was unanimous and binding.

We are either going to have compliance with international law or nonexistence. The United States and Israel are aware of their responsibility to comply with these resolutions and are flaunting international law at the expenses of civilians in both Palestine and Israel.

The millions of Jews who oppose the Israeli government's policy of state terror are not anti-Semites. People who hate Arabs are anti-Semites. People who hate Jews are anti-Semites.

A Hopeful Future:
The United Republic
of the Middle East 2020

April 22, 2002

The present government of the United Republic of the Middle East was formed after much unnecessary pain and suffering. The cause of over a half-century of war is identified as an outdated attempt to manipulate politics under the banner of religion. Separatism in an age of globalized solidarity was counterproductive to any hope of human rights and social justice. Palestinians formed an inter-religious unity among their Christian and Islamic people. Israel identified its fundamentalists as an obstacle to unity comparing them to both Christian and Islamic fanatics. The Israeli peace movement became a majority denouncing nuclear weapons and militarism as clearly suicidal. Israel joined the Republic together with Palestine.

If demagogical religious manipulation continued, it was clear that Sunni would fight Shiia forever so Iran and Iraq became members of the United Republic of the Middle East. Jordan was quick to join the Union, as was Lebanon with a mix of Maronite Christians, Islamics and Druse. Syria did not want to become an international ghetto, so it joined the union as did the family states of Saudi Arabia and Kuwait. The birth of this new republic in 2020 was sparked as the Israeli people rejected the continuing military oppression of Palestine. Islamic states also accepted the conviction that religion cannot be the basis of a functional polity.

History proves that such efforts only lead to inquisition, exclusion and violence. Non-Zionist Jews rejoiced in the realization that they would no longer be marginalized from their ethnicity by a nineteenth century ideology. Non-religious Jews, Islamics and Christians rejoiced to know that they would no longer have their lives curtailed by religious taboos. Millions of Islamic, Jewish and Christian women celebrated their new-found equal rights with men.

The constitution of the United Republic of the Middle East is no longer based on disputed sacred texts. Separation of Church and State became a reality which protects the practice of all religions:

> The parliament shall make no law respecting an establishment of religion, or prohibiting the free exercise thereof: or abridging the freedom of speech, or of the press; or the right of people peaceably to assemble, and to petition the government for redress of grievances.

The new republic borrowed the First Amendment of the Constitution of the United States of America. Another component was borrowed from Article Six of the Constitution, Section Three; "No religious test shall ever be required as a qualification to any office or public trust under the United Republic of the Middle East."

Contemporary polities must be based on social justice and human rights. Public policy is properly derived from sociology, not religious doctrine. What about the Holy City of the three Abrahamic religions, Islam, Judaism and Christianity? Jerusalem remains and as international shrine to the separation of church and state. Just think only eighteen years ago, in 2002, the Middle East was enmeshed in the politics of terror and hysteria. Today, in 2020, it is a functional and prosperous United Republic of the Middle East, which rejoices in religious freedom and tolerance. If this new republic had not been visualized, it never would have become a reality.

The Marches of April 20, 2002

April 29, 2002

Just over a week ago we gathered at San Francisco's Dolores Park at 11:00 A.M. By noon, the park was a sea of people and we began our march to the Civic Center in that beautiful city. Literally hundreds of organizations were present. But what made this march one of historic significance? It was conducted simultaneously with a march three times its size taking place in Washington, D.C.

People whose sole source of information is the commercial media would not be aware that the current peace movement is even larger than the movement during the Vietnam War. Why? Because the commercial media has chosen to ignore much of the current peace movement. In Los Angeles for example, a gathering of 5,000 people for peace was judged as a non-happening. Only those who were passing on the street . . . or those in the march itself or those who listen to Pacifica might know the depth of this movement . . .

But this is not all . . .

The current peace movement is to be found in every community in the United States . . . it is now to be found in every religious body as well. The conspiracy of silence can go on no longer.

And there is something even more profound about the historic nature of the San Francisco and Washington marches. Aside from the issue relating to America's new policy of eternal war, these were the biggest demonstrations in solidarity with the Palestinian people in U.S. history and a repudiation of the shameful legacy of silence.

In the light of the oppression and summary arrest of people in the United States since September 11, 2001, it is truly striking that so many tens of thousands of Arab-American, South Asian and Muslim communities appeared in the United States in this period of warmongering frenzy and governmental suppression. They know that many of their colleagues are held without trial in U.S. prisons but they were there. These communities had been demonized as terrorists. Thousands have been illegally detained, tens of thousands have been visited by the FBI.

These marches were historic, therefore, because the plight of the Palestinians has not been part of the mainstream peace movement in the United States.

Back in 1967, the same movement that supported the struggle against apartheid in South Africa and opposed the war in Vietnam did not respond strongly to the seizure of the West Bank, Gaza, the Golan Heights and the Sinai. Similarly, when a million people opposed nuclear weapons in New York City on June 12, 1982, there was no condemnation of the Israeli invasion of Lebanon that had begun just a week before. Twenty-thousand Lebanese and Palestinian people eventually died during that invasion as the Israeli defense forces led by General Ariel Sharon drove Yassir Arafat and the Palestine Liberation Movement from Beirut.

Yes, the marches in April in San Francisco and Washington, D.C. were historic for the above reason but there is even more. The Israeli peace movement is stronger than ever.

Men and women in black, Palestinians and Israelis are marching together, not only in San Francisco and Washington, but in Tel Aviv. Yes, today Israelis and Palestinians are marching for peace at the very moment when tanks and helicopters are striking Hebron.

International solidarity that knows of no borders continues to arrive in Palestine by way of Doctors Without Borders, Voices in the Wilderness and a host of people from around the globe.

Israeli peace people bring food and medicine to suffering Palestinians at the very time that the internationals are bringing such aid to the people in the Church of the Nativity in Bethlehem.

Israel's singer of war songs, Yaffa Yarkoni, has refused to sing in the face of the oppression. The Israeli peace movement is saying exactly what we are saying in the United States. In a report today from Israel, the spokesperson said that "Jewish Israelis don't know what is going on in the occupied territories," and we can add that the people of the United States are similarly deprived.

There is no vitality in the forces of oppression. This is not a fight between Israel and Palestine. If it were, there would not be so many people from both sides marching together. This is a fight for the human race, which is on the verge of destroying itself by ignorance, violence and vengeance.

History is being made by the people marching for justice and peace in the U.S., in Israel, in Palestine and throughout the world.

Let us abolish the war system and establish a peace system.

The Coming Disaster in Iraq

May 6, 2002

Mr. Cheney has been going door to door throughout the Middle East, saying to each head of state, "Will you help us blow up Iraq?" And he comes home pouting that no one understands him and his apocalyptic vision of eternal war. All of the heads of state said, "No, we will not." Just like Rodney Dangerfield, Cheney got no respect.

The heads of state with whom Cheney met have no love of Saddam Hussein. And while we are at it, please identify any head of state for whom you have a special love. If every disliked head of state were bombed, there would probably be no existing states in the world.

But Cheney was on a mission authorized by Mr. Bush, who is handled by addicts of war. (By the way, I recommend the new comic book entitled, *Addicted to War*. Our young people will learn more about the cult of militarism in this short and accurate book by Joel Andreas than they might learn in their first twelve years of schooling).

I was in Iraq in January of 1991, just before all hell broke loose. We spent a day in Babylon in that cradle of civilization and then returned to Baghdad in the evening. There were ten of us and our minibus wound its way into the neighborhood of the diplomatic community. We were escorted into a home to find that dinner was ready and Yasser Arafat was the surprise guest. Yasser Arafat was despondent because President Bush, the elder, would not talk to him, as he assured everyone that he could negotiate a peace with Saddam Hussein and that the upcoming war would be a lose/lose situation.

Mikhail Gorbachev was also trying to avoid this unnecessary war. But the long-standing friend and ally of our government, Saddam Hussein, had committed the unforgivable sin of nationalizing Iraq's oil and that was judged to be against corporate interests . . . therefore, Saddam was dubbed as Adolph Hitler. Someone seems to have forgotten that we supported Iraq and Saddam Hussein against Iran in the 1980s in one of the major wars of the 20th century.

Since 1991 we have bombed Iraq on what Mr. Bush, the younger, calls "routine missions." Just like routine drive-by shootings. We have also had a routine embargo, that is destroying the children of Iraq.

But Iraq has weapons of mass destruction! Well, well . . . and we don't have such weapons? The selectivity of our concerns is overwhelming.

But mindless Republican and Democratic legislators, together with the commercial media, are salivating for new kills in Iraq. Thanks to former Attorney General Ramsey Clark, our endless attacks on Iraq are designated as war crimes. No wonder we want to unsign our pledge to support an International Criminal Court.

Yes, in the absence of an International Criminal Court, the former Attorney General conducted hearings in twenty nations and thirty cities in the United States. This International War Crimes Tribunal was concluded on Saturday, February 29, 1992 in New York City. I was one of hundreds of eyewitnesses who testified at these hearings. The Tribunal's international panel of judges concluded that President George Bush was guilty of nineteen charges brought against him by the Commission of Inquiry.

Here is Charge Number Ten: "President Bush obstructed justice and corrupted United Nations functions as a means of securing power." The evidence to support this charge was overwhelming. It included both bribes and threats.

The same newspapers, which publish today's warmongering editorials, refused to cover the decision of the International War Crimes Tribunal and were thereby guilty of a breach of their professional responsibility to the public. The foreign press covered the Tribunal as an important news story and was present as an international panel of twenty-two judges gave the pronouncement of guilt before an audience of 1,500 people in New York.

The 5,000 to 6,000 deaths caused monthly by the combination of bomb damage and United Nations sanctions are a continuing crime against humanity. The sanctions are killing infants, children, the sick, and the elderly. Actually, there was no war in Iraq. There was only a merciless slaughter conducted by 110,000 aerial sorties dropping 88,000 tons of explosives. 93% of these explosives fell freely on a defenseless country.

We must stop the maniacal plan of a renewed war in Iraq. Such a plan recklessly endangers the people of the United States.

The Third Reich acknowledged its unspeakable horrors and Germany has developed into a peaceful and productive nation. It seems that the time is right for us to acknowledge our misdeeds as well. Confession is good for the soul.

A New Dimension

May 15, 2002

The division of politics into left and right is an extremely shallow concept. Actually, there is nothing linear about political, social and economic convictions.

As an example, one of the largest peace demonstrations in Israeli history took place this week. The commercial media referred to Israeli "leftists" demonstrating in Tel Aviv. But to understand what occurred in Israel we must look to a third dimension . . . not a simple line.

The third dimension includes the moral and ethical, indeed, it includes the spiritual. Both so-called left and right can be violent and unethical. But the third dimension includes reconciliation, non-violence and repentance.

Ethical praxis evolves into a spiritual reality where reconciliation and peace are possible. Useless and counter-productive militarism simply expands the path of vengeance and hatred. Indeed ethics must be the compass for economic and political decisions.

Rather than using the word "leftist," the media could have made reference to people of conscience, ethics and spirit who led that Israeli march. These blessed souls actually held back an attack on the nearly defenseless people of Gaza.

So it is that words like leftist and terrorist have been misused for political purposes. People of conscience and spirit know that the war is the crime. They have had enough of the nonsense promoted by the last refuge of scoundrels.

Both sides are mired in violence. Neither side is correct. Oh, yes, one side can be identified as the oppressed and one as the oppressor. That is true. But reconciliation must still be the goal, not vengeance.

The marches of April 20 in the United States were the largest expression of empathy with the Palestinian cause in the history of the United States. Jews, Christians, Muslims and many other faiths expressed that empathy. Thousands of miles away, the massive expression of tens of thousands of peace people of in Tel Aviv was equally historic and

24

meaningful.

These international marches are not conducted by naïve people. The marchers know that if existing International Law had been obeyed . . . there would have been no further bloodshed between Palestine and Israel.

We are now ready for a deepening of that third dimension in the United States. We wish to propose marches of approximately 50% representing the people of Israel together with 50% representing the people of Palestine. Such marches could be led by two coffins, one draped with the Israeli flag and the other draped with the Palestinian flag. The marches will be for justice, peace, reconciliation and compliance with existing International Law. Elected officials of all kinds should be at the head of these marches. They should have no fear of leaning to either side. We need no further slogans than justice, peace, reconciliation and law.

Would some knee-jerk media types call such a march "leftist?" I suppose they could. But I believe the rest of the community would get the idea.

The Disgrace of the AFL-CIO

May 22, 2002

As a member of the AFL-CIO College Faculty Guild, I wish to object to the foreign policy of our union. For years we were subject to the embarrassment of the American Institute for Free Labor Development known as AIFLD. AIFLD was internationally known as a CIA labor front that was dedicated to subverting independent militant unions and provoking labor unrest in governments at variance with Washington.

And now AIFLD has changed its name to the American Center for International Labor Solidarity or ACILS, which was recently providing aid and technical advisors to the Confederation of Venezuelan Workers. That's right . . . ACILS was one of the key participants in the recent attempt to overthrow president Hugo Chavez in Venezuela. The Confederation of Venezuelan Workers joined with the largest business association in Venezuela to organize the anti-government march on the Presidential Palace. More than a dozen people were shot to death and most of them were Chavez supporters.

The leader of the business group, Pedro Carmona Estanga was proclaimed President and he quickly ordered the disbanding of the national legislature, the elimination of the Constitution and the repeal of all laws passed during the previous four years of Hugo Chavez' presidency.

AFILD, became internationally known as a CIA front and was operative in organizing compliant company unions among the banana workers in Guatemala, it assisted company unions in Brazil to help the military seize power in 1964, it aided the 1973 coup in Chile by supporting a strike of the truck drivers leading to the take-over of General Augosto Pinocet Ugarte, it worked in El Salvador to build a pro-military peasant association under the guise of land reform which was modeled on the counterinsurgency programs of the Vietnam War.

The cosmetic change of name for AIFLD came with John Sweeney who inherited the personnel and world wide offices as the group was christened with a new name, The American Center for International Labor Solidarity.

So ACILS is a clone of AIFLD. A rose by any other name still smells sweet and the same applies to things that are foul smelling.

How similar all of this is to the situation at the School of the Americas? Just as the terrorist training camp at Fort Benning, Georgia has changed its name to the Western Hemisphere Institute for Security and Cooperation with the hope that Congress would not hold it responsible for the School of the Americas' lethal record . . . so the disgraceful history of AIFLD is covered by changing its name.

As a member of the AFL-CIO College Faculty Guild, I object to the foreign policy of our union and I urge all members and non-members to do the same.

Pledge of Resistance

May 30, 2002

A pledge of Resistance is circulating around the country and I would like to share it with you. Thousands of people will be taking this pledge on June 6th of this year. Perhaps you would like to join them.

The *Not in Our Name* project draws strength and inspiration from the anti-war and anti-repression movements.

The *Not in Our Name* project is being developed to strengthen and expand the existing movement of resistance.

This is the resistance of critical thought; resistance by speaking out, resistance by creating powerful art in finding ways to halt the machinery of war. This is resistance by individuals and resistance through mass action. The web site for *Not in Our Name* is: www.notinourname.net

We encourage everyone to take up the Pledge of Resistance declaring their determination to resist the addicts of perpetual war. We must dare to change the course of history. We are not here to watch history; we are here to participate in the making of history.

And here I quote the Pledge of Resistance:

We believe that as people living in the United States
it is our responsibility
to resist the injustices
done by our government, in our names.

Not in our name
will you wage "endless war"
there can be no more deaths
no more transfusions of blood for oil.

Not in our name
will you invade countries
bomb civilians, kill more children

letting history take its course
over the graves of the nameless.
Not in our name
will you erode the very freedoms
you've claimed to fight for.

Not by our hands
will we supply weapons and funding
for the annihilation of families
on foreign soil.

Not by our mouths
Will we let fear silence us.

Not by our hearts
will we allow whole peoples
or countries to be deemed evil.

Not by our will
And not in our name.

We pledge resistance
we pledge alliance with those
who have come under attack
for voicing opposition to the war
or for their religion or ethnicity.

We pledge to make common cause
with the people of the world
to bring about justice and peace.

Another world is possible
and we pledge to make it real.

Korea

June 6, 2002

The war in Korea is not over, only a cease-fire prevents the outbreak of another catastrophic blood bath. This is why Koreans on both sides of the 38th parallel want to replace the 1953 armistice with a peace treaty. In the meantime, 37,000 U.S. troops remain in Korea, one of the world's most highly militarized locations.

Who started the war in Korea? The official story is that it began with an attack by North Korea on orders from the Kremlin. But the Korean War was not the result of an outbreak of fighting early in the morning of June 25, 1950. Actually the peninsula had been in armed conflict for several years. In May of 1949, South Korea launched several battalions in an attack on North Korea. Only by claiming that North Korea invaded South Korea could the US send troops under the United Nations Flag. The question of who started the war was critical to obtain this UN cover. If South Korea was found to have initiated hostilities during the incident of May, 1949 the UN Charter would have required that South Korea be censured as the aggressor and any subsequent UN intervention would have been directed at defending North Korea from further aggression.

One must look at the work of I.F. Stone and his *Hidden History of the Korean War* for a detailed understanding of how the U.S. falsely claimed that North Korea attacked first. The Korean War was triggered by Syngman Rhee with behind the scenes support of John Foster Dulles. Rhee wanted to rule over all of Korea and called for reunification through military means.

Fifty-five thousand American lives were sacrificed in the Korean War; 3,000,000 Koreans and Chinese were killed. Every city in North Korea was bombed to total destruction. Just as in Vietnam, our administration could never clearly explain to the GI's why they were sent to Korea. The troops never understood why they should go to an impoverished land and kill people who knew neither communism nor democracy and who really wanted to be left alone. The only sensible words were heard by General Omar Bradley who stated that the Korean War was a "wrong war against a wrong enemy at the wrong place in the wrong time."

Lies and deception also took the lives of 3,000,000 people in Vietnam a few years later. The most common remark from Vietnam Veterans is, "I was lied to." Albert Einstein stated that the US had manipulated the UN for its own benefit. He went on to say that great powers do not act on the basis of facts but only manufacture facts to serve their purposes and force their will on smaller nations.

And now is the time for Americans to stand with the Korean people in their struggle for reunification and reconciliation. Continuing misinformation from Washington can lead us to resume our 52 year old war with the possibility of a U.S. first strike nuclear disaster.

Quite simply, empire never learns because it operates on power and considers truth to be irrelevant. That is why the ignorance and malice of the Korean War was repeated in Vietnam, Central America, Iraq and Afghanistan.

We must stop before we kill again!
The first casualty of war is truth.

Preemptive Doctrine

June 20, 2002

Shoot first, ask questions later. That's the new doctrine of preemption coming from Mr. Bush by way of his War Department handlers. Preemption is the ultimate unilateral action. George Bush alone reserves the right to determine what constitutes a threat to US security and to act even if that threat is not judged to be imminent.

All of the pain imposed on Iraq simply because they refuse to privatize their oil industry production. How quickly the world's leaders caught on to the new Bush Doctrine. Only days after the doctrine of preemption was announced we heard Mr. Sharon talking about preemptive strikes against Palestine.

India can now use a preemptive nuclear strike to stop any threats from Pakistan. China can now use preemption to justify an attack on Taiwan. But wait, preemption is not a new policy at all . . . it is a very old and a very tired policy. Was not Grenada was on the verge of invading the United States in 1983? But Ronald Reagan preempted that by sending in the 82nd airborne and bombing their mental hospital.

Was not Nicaragua on the verge of invading the United States in the 1980s when the same preemptor saved us by illegally forming a mercenary army to devastate that country?

Did not Mr. Nixon save us from the possibility of democracy in Chile in 1973 by preempting Salvador Allende and imposing the Nazi Dictator Augusto Pinochet? How, then, can we preempt war insanity and addiction? We must not cooperate with these endless provocations and join the rest of the world in the quest for justice and peace.

We must join forces with voices of reason. Our country is incapable of delivering health care or education on a par with France or Italy as our taxes are being wasted on run away militarism. We have yet to see Mr. Bush make his first step to assist the domestic needs of the people of the United States. His every step so far has simply increased our endangerment.

The most serious perilous act of preemptive policy is the executive's determination to make first strike nuclear attacks against other nations whether they have nuclear weapons or not. Unbelievably Mr. Bush has broken away from the 1972 Antiballistic Missile Treaty.

All right, what is to be done? Simply call 202-224-3121 and ask for your representative's office. Tell your representative to support the lawsuit of Representative Dennis Kucinich and 30 other members of the House of Representatives who are suing the President seeking a temporary restraining order to stop the pullout of the United States from the 1972 Antiballistic Missile Treaty.

Just make that call. I think we can preempt Mr. Bush on this one.

Dr. Nurit Peled-Elhanan

June 27, 2002

Here are selected words from a mother who lost her daughter in Israel. She is Dr. Nurit Peled-Elhanan:

> In the place that I come from, Death has dominion. And it is Death that has created a new identity for me and has given me the voice of our biblical mother Rachel, weeping for her children, refusing to be comforted for they are not.
>
> My little girl was killed just because she was born Israeli, by a young man who felt hopeless to the point of murder and suicide just because he was born a Palestinian.
>
> For me, the other side is not the Palestinians. For me the whole population of the area, and of the world has always been divided into two other distinct groups: peace lovers and war lovers.
>
> I believe very strongly that only by educating our children that killing the innocent, starving the innocent, and humiliating the innocent are unforgivable crimes, can we save them from joining the evil forces that are luring them.
>
> But terrorism dominates both forces. An organized army, which terrorizes a whole population, is no less and even more criminal than any guerrilla group. An enlightened first world government which ordains the killing of the innocent is just as evil as any third world guerrilla leader who is hardly known and never seen. There is no enlightened killing and barbaric killing, there is only criminal killing.
>
> For me, Saddam Hussein and Ariel Sharon and George Bush, father and son, are all the same, for they have all inflicted pain and death upon innocent populations. If we don't tell our children these are unscrupulous murderers, we shall never have people who rule out killing from the outset as a solution to social and political problems.
>
> Ending the war means to adopt a dialogic approach to negotiation to understand that people should talk not in order to bring the others to their knees and win the argument, but in order to come to terms. Ending the war means that I don't care what flag is put on which mountain, it means

that I don't care who looks where or when they pray, it means that nothing is more important than to secure a little girl's way to her dance class.

I would like to call all the parents who have not yet lost their children, and all those who are about to, if we don't stand up to the politicians by teaching our children not to follow their murderous ways, if we don't listen to the voice of peace coming from underneath, very soon there will be nothing left to say, nothing left to write or read or listen to except for the perpetual cry of mourning. Please, save the children.

Full Text Follows:

Thank you for inviting me to share with you the struggle for peace in my country. I say MY country but I don't even know if this term is correct anymore. What exactly is mine in this country depends very much on what I identify with, and today it is a very difficult for me to answer that; for it is very hard to identify with anything in a place that has let Death have dominion over it. And in the place that I come from, Death has dominion. And it is Death that has created a new identity for me and has given me a new voice, a new voice that is as ancient as the world itself the voice of our biblical mother Rachel, weeping for her children, refusing to be comforted for they are not. This new identity and this new voice transcends nationalities, religions and even time and over-shadows all other identities and is deafening all the other voices I have been given by life.

My little girl was killed just because she was born Israeli, by a young man who felt hopeless to the point of murder and suicide just because he was born a Palestinian. After her death, a reporter asked me how I can accept condolences from the other side. I said to her very spontaneously, that I do not accept condolences from the other side. And when the mayor of Jerusalem came to offer his condolences, I went to my room because I didn't want to speak to him or shake his hand. Because for me, the other side is not the Palestinians, and I believe that dividing the population into two enemy sides, Palestinians and Israelis, is a wrong and a murderous division. For me, the whole population of the area, and of the world has always been divided into two other distinct groups: peace lovers and war lovers.

But today I know that there is yet another division in Israel: On the face of the earth there rules the kingdom of evil, where for the last 34 years, people who call themselves leaders have earned, through democratic means, the right to kill and destroy and be as vile and corrupt as they please; to have young boys become expert killers, whether in the name of God, of the good of the nation, or in the name of honour and of courage. But these evil people have created yet another kingdom, a glorious kingdom that flourishes and grows larger and larger every day—a kingdom that lives and breathes under our feet, under the earth we walk on. There is where my little daughter dwells, side by side with Palestinian children, and where I dwell side by side with Palestinian parents who, for the most part, have never held a gun and have never obeyed orders to kill anyone. There she dwells, alongside her murderer, whose blood is mingled with hers on the stones of Jerusalem that have long grown indifferent to human blood. There they lie, both of them, deceived.

He is deceived, because his act of murder and suicide did not change anything, did not end the Israeli cruel occupation, did not bring him to heaven; and the people who promised him that his act would be meaningful carry on as if he had never existed. My little girl is deceived because she believed that her life was safe, that her parents and her country were protecting her from evil and that no harm can come to little girls who are good and gentle, and go through the streets of their own cities, to a dance class.

And they are both deceived because the world is going on living as if their blood has never been shed. Both of them are the victims of their so-called leaders. And those so-called leaders keep on enjoying playing their murderous games, using our children as their puppets, and our grief as an incentive to go on with their vindictive tricks. For them, children are abstract entities and numbers and grief is a political tool. They know that all they have to do in order to draw more and more young and enthusiastic little soldiers into their units is to find a God that would ordain this killing. And each of them finds Him in their own bible, in their own mythologies. They commit their crimes in the name of the Jewish God and in the name of the Muslim God, while in Ireland and in Eastern Europe people kill each other for different versions of their Christian God. And now the enlightened leaders of the West kill in the name of the God of Freedom. But in fact, they all recruit man-made gods to their sides - the God of racism and the God of greed and megalomania.

This is not new in the history of man. People have always used God as an excuse for their crimes. Our children, from a very tender age learn about Joshua, the glorified leader who murdered the whole population of Jericho in the name of God. Then they learn about the prophet Eliyahu who killed the 450 priests of the Baal because they practiced a different religion and then they learn about Eliyahu's disciple, Elisha, who brought death, with the help of God, upon 42 children who mocked him by calling him bald. Not to mention the adored King David and his terrible deeds. In our culture that allows killing as a means of solving

36

social and religious problems, and where people identify themselves with biblical heroes and see themselves as their descendants, all these stories are glorified and overshadow the story about the God who said "Lay not thy hand upon the child."

But children can also learn about the God who said "I will have mercy upon her who have not obtained mercy and I will say to them who were not my people 'Thou art my people.'" I believe very strongly that only by educating our children that killing the innocent, starving the innocent, and humiliating the innocent are unforgivable crimes, we can save them from joining the evil forces of Israel and Palestine that are luring them into their lines. Unfortunately, Israel, through its long and cruel occupation, is making it very easy for young Palestinians to turn to the way of terrorism. But terrorism dominates both forces. An organized army, which terrorizes a whole population, is no less and even more criminal than any guerrilla group. An enlightened first world government which ordains the killing of the innocent is just as evil as any third world guerrilla leader who is hardly known and never seen.

There is no enlightened killing and barbaric killing, there is only criminal killing. For me, Saddam Hussein and Ariel Sharon and George Bush, father and son, are all the same; for they have all inflicted pain and death upon innocent populations. If we don't tell our children these are unscrupulous murderers, we shall never have people who rule out killing from the outset as a solution to social and political problems. Today, when there is no opposition in Israel, there is no more meaning to left or right, for they all give their consent to the atrocities that occur in this country. Therefore, I believe that the European condemnation if those deeds and of their doers is highly important.

It is time to tell the world that words like heroism, courage, and manhood can kill and that the death of one child, any child, be it a Serbian or an Albanian, an Iraqi or a Jewish child is the death of the whole world, its past and its future. That there is no vengeance for the death of a child because after the death of a child there is no other death—for there is no more life. And where there is no more life there are no more words left to love or hate with, and the only sound that reverberates in this arena of death is the helpless cry of dying children and of bereaved mothers.

This is the cry that has never, never been heard by politicians and generals, especially not in a Jerusalem that everybody thinks is made of gold but that is really made of stones and iron and lead. It is time this cry is heard above all others, for this is the only voice that remains after the violence, and that really understands the meaning of the end of all things, including wars. This is the voice that understands what today is understood

37

only in the underground kingdom of our murdered children, namely that all bloods are equal and that it takes so little to kill a child and so much to keep her alive. It understands that ending the war means to adopt a dialogic approach to negotiation and not a smart dealer approach, to understand that people should talk, not in order to bring the others to their knees and win the argument, but in order to come to terms. Ending the war means that I don't care what flag is put on which mountain, it means that I don't care who looks where when they pray, it means that nothing is more important than to secure a little girl's way to her dance class.

I would like to call all the parents who have not yet lost their children, and all those who are about to, if we don't stand up to the politicians by teaching our children not to follow their murderous ways, if we don't listen to the voice of peace coming from underneath, very soon there will be nothing left to say, nothing left to write or read or listen to except for the perpetual cry of mourning. Please, save the children.

Palestine

July 2, 2002

How many times does government policy truly represent the wishes of its people? I would say, rarely. When we hear of some new, vicious and vengeful policy, our question in conscience is always, "Are we not better than that?" I see no reason why governments cannot act in the same spirit as movements of international solidarity.

As we examine the make up of the solidarity affinity groups in Palestine, we find that a substantial percent of the activists are either Jewish internationals or Israelis. The relationship between Palestinians and solidarity Israelis is one of warmth and respect. It is similar to the relationship between the African Americans and the thousands of white citizens who ventured to the south in the midst of the Civil Rights movement.

The Israeli press refers to Gaza as a large prison. A third of the area was taken over by some 7,000 Israeli settlers. The remainder is home to a million Palestinians. Where do Palestinians get food? Some 80% of Gaza's residents depend on their sustenance from The United Nations, the European Union, or other sources of international relief.

The majority of Palestinians will only be able to maintain a reasonable life through the help of international aid. The current Israeli plan is to return to the concept of military administration as during the pre-Oslo years. The destruction of the Palestinian authority began in April of this year. From that time on, the towns and villages of the West Bank have been completely sealed. Even exit by foot, which was previously possible, is now blocked. Soldiers and snipers prevent any unauthorized walking into agricultural fields to places of work, study or medical treatment.

Why is Israel pressuring the European Union to stop its aid to Palestine? This aid includes the salaries of teachers and health workers. The Israeli government is also on a campaign to defund the UN aid program of 400 million dollars per year that is feeding the town and cities of Palestine during the current siege.

Prime Minister Sharon continues an analogy between the occupied territories and the war in Afghanistan. The analogy is revealing; at the outset of the US war with Afghanistan, the U.S. demanded that Pakistan stop truck convoys of food and fuel to the Afghani people during our siege of that country.

Afghanistan was on a lifeline and we just cut the lifeline. We must insist that Palestine continue to receive food and medical aid from the United Nations, from the European Union or from any other nations, civic groups, church or private sources.

This is also a critical moment to keep our eyes open for any misguided members of the U.S. Congress or administration who are attempting to support starvation tactics of forbidding food and medical aid to Palestine. Starving a people is no way to create a just and lasting peace.

Dr. Martin Luther King and Rabbi Michael Lerner

July 10, 2002

When Dr. Martin Luther King spoke at Riverside Church on April 4, 1967 he referred to his country as, "the greatest purveyor of violence in the world today." Dr. King was speaking of the military take over of the United States of America. That military take over is reflected in the run away waste and environmental destruction of limitless military adventures and expenditures. That military take over is obvious in the absolute lack of diplomacy in our dealings with other nations.

That military take over is obvious in our open plans to massacre civilians in Iraq. That military take over is clear as our nation is incapable of delivering adequate health care and public education. Dr. King said, "A nation that continues year after year to spend more money on military defense than on programs of social uplift is approaching spiritual death."

Just as Dr. Martin Luther King was considered anti-Christian by many reactionary Christians in 1967, so some of his fellow religionists consider Rabbi Michael Lerner to be outside the pale in 2002.

Here are some of Rabbi Lerner's thoughts to compare and contrast with those of Dr. King:

We are outraged by the immoral acts of Palestinian terrorists who blow up Israelis at Seder tables, or while they shop, or sit in cafes, or ride on buses. Hundreds of thousands of Palestinians fled their homes in 1948, and recent research by Israeli historians has shown most fled not because they were responding to the appeal of Arab leaders but because they feared acts of violence by right wing Israeli terrorists or were forced from their homes by the Israeli army. Palestinian refugees and their families now number more than 3 million, and many live in horrifying conditions in refugee camps under Israeli military rule. Sharon has always opposed any deal that would involve abandoning the West Bank settlements, which he helped to expand in the 1980's precisely to insure that Israel would never give up the occupied territories.

41

Sharon recently set out to destroy the institutions of Palestinian society and has done so with murderous brutality with little regard for human rights and with great harm to many civilians.

Non-Jews are doing no favors to the Jewish people when, by their silence, they help the most destructive elements of the Jewish world pursue immoral policies that almost certainly will generate more hatred of Jews.

Thank you, Dr. King and Rabbi Lerner.

Iraq Peace Team

July 19, 2002

Those who identify powerful instruments of change that are civilized, strong and effective deserve to be remembered. We will imitate them for centuries to come. Those who use the barbaric instruments of change of the past, including the current mindless cabal in Washington, certainly deserve to be forgotten as soon as possible. Let's take a look at an announcement from the Iraq Peace Team, which is a project of Voices in the Wilderness:

> When and if it appears that war against Iraq is at hand, we will go to Iraq with these intentions:
>
> - We will live among the Iraqi people.
>
> - We will be with the Iraqi people during any aggression directed at them, including continued economic sanctions.
>
> - We will use our presence and non-violent actions to protect, if we can, both the civilian population of Iraq and those facilities (for example water purification plants), which make daily life possible for the Iraqi people.
>
> - We will use our experiences to speak truthfully, from Iraq and through supporters in the U.S., to all who listen about the effects of sanctions and war on the people of Iraq.
>
> - We as a team do not take the side of any government, none of whom we consider blameless, and all of whom we ask to initiate dialogue and negotiation, especially under the auspices of the Secretary General of the United Nations. As peace minded people, we deplore all human rights violations, including those inherent in Security Council sanctions that have been imposed on the Iraqi people for eleven years.

Many of us have spent years working to end the economic sanctions against Iraq and have visited those in Iraq most affected by the sanctions. We have seen the grievous and enduring results of the 1991 war and the bombing by the United States and the United Kingdom that has continued since then. We have visited the hospitals and schools in many areas of Iraq. At home, we have done what we can to end the embargo and to advocate the beginnings of disarmament throughout the entire region.

Iraq

July 29, 2002

Any incompetent can start a war. It requires humanity and genius to avoid one. Washington's social psychosis is more and more obvious to the world's intellectual community. On the centennial of the Nobel Prize, over 100 Nobel Laureates, primarily from the hard sciences called for the "replacement of war by law" and an end to "the unilateral search for security." The laureates called the performance of the corporate media, "a madman rhetoric." And referred to the situation of the world's poor as "desperate and manifestly unjust."

Just think about the level of cult mind control that has been accomplished by the media/government nexus. We have been psychically dulled to the point of calmly yielding as our President and our Congress are planning the cold-blooded murder of countless civilians in Iraq. This is to be done with knowledge and aforethought.

And what is the motive for this planned massacre? The motive is to cover up their criminal performance at home and to silence the people of the United States with new and unacceptable limits on civil liberties and social justice. Quite simply, they are afraid of the people of the United States who are sick and tired of the government's inability to deliver such essentials as health care, education and a civil society. Oh, yes, there is a question of oil. But oil is only a symptom of deeper problems.

The Senate Foreign Relations Committee is under the control of Democratic Senator Joseph Biden. Biden is bringing people to speak to the Senate who are experts in nothing but war mongering, people like Paul Wolfowitz and Richard Perle. These are simply drum beaters for the upcoming massacre.

Authentic experts are being excluded from Biden's hearings. People like Scott Ritter, a chief UN weapons inspector in Iraq who says that Senator Joe Biden is running a sham hearing with a pre-ordained conclusion in order to provide a political cover for a massive military attack on Iraq.

Also excluded are: Dennis Halliday who called our plans "genocidal"

45

and as an inspector said that Iraq did not have weapons of mass destruction; Mr. Hans von Sponeck, former Assistant Secretary General of the United Nations, who resigned his post as Coordinator of Humanitarian Aid in Iraq so he could freely speak out about the destruction of that country.

Biden might even call upon George Bush, Sr. who is aware of the war crimes he committed and how they led to his failure to be reelected. Biden should also call upon the U.S. Generals who are saying that Iraq is not a threat to the United States. Any incompetent can start a war. It takes humanity and genius to avoid one.

Lori Berenson

August 7, 2002

The Inter-American Commission on Human Rights of the Organization of American States has vindicated Lori Berenson. It has ruled that Peru's authoritarian laws instituted by the now disgraced former President Alberto Fujimori are illegal and violate fundamental human rights as specified by the American Convention on Human Rights.

This ruling was a very powerful condemnation of Peru at every level. Lori has never had a trial that respected her rights or met international standards of fairness and due process. She was charged under the antiterrorist laws that the Inter-American Commission has said are unacceptable. And she has been incarcerated under conditions that are inhumane and degrading. Unfortunately, despite this ruling, Lori continues to be held in a remote mountain prison because Peru refuses to act responsibly and abide by its international human rights commitments. Instead, Peru has chosen the unprecedented step of suing the Inter-American Commission at the Inter-American Court of Human Rights.

We are sure the Inter-American Court will also vindicate Lori. Lori is innocent of the charges that were used to sentence her on two separate occasions in illegal court procedures under internationally condemned laws. She has never been charged with a violent act. She first faced a kangaroo court in the form of a hooded military tribunal in 1995. Her retrial in 2000, which was highly touted in Peru as "fair," was nothing more than a show trial, now condemned by the Inter-American Commission. This November will mark seven years of wrongful imprisonment for Lori. She spent nearly three years at the internationally condemned Yanamayo Prison in the southern Andes where the bitter cold and 12,700 feet altitude severely impaired her health. She later endured months of solitary confinement at Socabaya Prison until Amnesty International, the Catholic Church and the International Committee of the Red Cross intervened.

On December 21, 2001, she was physically and sexually abused when moved to Huacariz Prison in the northern Andes. And now that the Peruvian government is waging an all out fight including an unprecedented legal attack on the Inter-American Commission, Lori must wait for the Inter-American Court decision.

This will mean more years of wrongful imprisonment and possible mistreatment unless the United States government acts forcefully.

Haiti

August 14, 2002

President Jean-Bertrand Aristide and the Government of Haiti endorsed the Initial Draft Accord proposed by the Organization of the American States (OAS) to the Haitian political parties, seeking an end to the political crisis that has halted the flow of international humanitarian and development assistance to Haiti. Haiti has once again demonstrated its willingness to end the crippling political impasse, which stemmed from the May 21, 2000 elections.

Under the Accord, the Government of Haiti will hold national elections in the second quarter of 2003 to replace members of Parliament who were elected on May 21, 2000. These members have agreed to sacrifice two years of their terms to end the crisis. Local officials would also be elected at this time. In addition to the election provision, the Initial Draft Accord addresses issues surrounding the December 17, 2001 attack on the National Palace in Port-au-Prince and the subsequent violence. The Government pledged to continue to "combat impunity and place the highest priority on strengthening judicial institutions."

In its endorsement of the Initial Draft Accord, the Government of Haiti agrees to pay reparations to any agencies, institutions, organizations and individuals that suffered damages in connection with the attack on the National Palace on December 17, 2001. President Aristide said, "The people of Haiti demand and urgently need an end to the political and economic crisis."

The United States is currently leading an economic embargo against Haiti and is withholding more than $500 million in humanitarian development assistance loans from the Inter-American Development Bank (IDB).

During many years of corrupt Haitian dictatorships we heard little condemnation of Haitian government. Now that Haiti is in a democratic process, our country is starving out one of the world's poorest countries and even demanding that Haiti pay interest on loans it has not received.

In order to save his people, Jean Bertrand Aristide is being forced to comply with implications that he is responsible the for violence and misery in Haiti. He needs our solidarity.

An Appeal to Bush and Cheney on the Anniversary of September 11

September 10, 2002

September 11, 2001 was a tragedy for the United States of America. It was a tragedy for the families of those who perished in Washington and in New York and Pennsylvania. It was a tragedy for thousands of victims of retaliation and vengeance against the people of Afghanistan who had no part whatsoever in the attacks on the United States.

And it was also a tragedy for the people of the United States who did not suffer directly from the attacks. Part of the tragedy is that an un-elected individual gained near dictatorial powers. Are you aware of the manic obsession that Bush and Cheney are demonstrating?

Have you ever wondered about their motivation? They can speak of nothing but starting a war when the whole world is telling them not to do this. The Generals are telling them not to do this. The Kissingers are telling them not to do this. The Scowcrofts are telling them not to do this. The UN weapons inspectors of Iraq are telling them not to do this. Republican Senators are telling them not to do this. The people of the United States are telling them not to do this.

Mr. Bush and Mr. Cheney, I have reviewed every possible reason for your intransigence on this matter. You have no right to conduct a first strike war of aggression against Iraq. Your repetitious babble and threats of slaughter against the Iraqi people are bankrupt. Your claims are a lie.

We lived with the Soviet Union for half a century without attacking them for their huge supply of weapons of mass destruction. Iraq has no such armaments as the former Soviet Union.

You are planning to put the finest of our young people in harms way. You are willing to see them come home in body bags. You are willing to kill even more Iraqi children than our illegal, immoral and terroristic policy has over the past 11 years.

Why are you demanding this blood bath?

Because your closest political advisers, your election advisers have explained to you that the Republican Party is going to lose in November if there is no war. Therefore, you are willing to preside over this slaughter to get your people reelected. This is impeachable Mr. Bush and Cheney. At first, I thought the reason might be oil alone. But if it were, you might get more support from your hawkish partisans.

No, oil is not enough of a reason. Iraq will sell you as much oil as you want. Once the American people understand your motives, and they understand them better every day, I think they will support your impeachment George Bush. You are not allowed to protect your position by plotting the death of our service people. Dick Cheney, you are not allowed to protect your financial behavior on the coffins of our service people.

The United States is in a condition of severe deterioration. Health facilities are closing, schools are shabby, unemployment is rampant. Exactly what have you done for the core needs of the people of the United States?

"There is No Peace Movement"

September 11, 2002

Yes, that year has passed.

Commendations to everyone who was not silenced by the trauma of the initial attack. Congratulations to everyone who took immediate action for a peaceful and just resolution of the crisis. I especially want to give thanks for the founders of the Coalition for World Peace who established themselves on September 12, 2001 and have been organizing every day for the past year.

When George Bush, Sr. unleashed 88,000 tons of bombs on the people of Iraq, he stated, "There is no peace movement." He was entirely wrong then and his son is entirely wrong today. At the time of the father there were international peace people all over Iraq documenting the terror of the U.S. attacks. History has the truth. The babble of corrupt politicians will not stand.

Sadly today there are some liberal minded people and even some ivory tower leftists who say there is no peace movement. Their problem is their dependence on commercial media and the commercial media is in a state of severe corporate censorship.

Look at the faces of the news anchors. They look like they are telling fairy tales to kindergarten children. Just how much can people prostitute themselves before they conclude that it is not worth the price?

Yes, there is a peace movement and it is wonderful to see the participation of the religious community. The Interfaith Communities United for Justice and Peace have been active during this troubled year. They have planned religious and educational events and are working together with the Coalition for World Peace. What a joy to see Rabbis, Imams, Priests, Ministers, Buddhists, Bahai's and Hindus working, praying and planning together with their conviction that religion must not bless war.

I know there is some talk about fascism, but let's not go there. Let's not have an abstract ideological discussion. Let's simply talk about the history of dictatorial practice in concrete terms.

Aside from visiting Iraq, I have lived in many Latin American dictatorships. One of the clear characteristics of dictatorships is the use of warm slogans. For example: "Fatherland, Family and Tradition; Kitchen, Children and Church." These are typical in the mix of dictatorial banter.

How about Homeland Security? Now that one sounds like the jargon of Augusto Pinochet Ugarte in Chile in 1973. Let's look at the logic. Let's look at the semantics. How about The Patriot Act? That one would sound good in Haiti during the days of Papa Doc Duvalier. It is designed to curtail civil liberties. And what about arbitrary detention of people and their substantive disappearance? That sounds like Guatemala under Rios Montt.

Homeland Security will close more medical centers in Los Angeles County. If it were truly security it would insist on maintaining the 15 health centers that are closing. As it is there will be countless preventatble deaths in Los Angeles county alone? This is security?

Friends, you must demand that your local legislators work for Homeland Security by demanding federal funds that have been stolen from health care. Don't let them cop out by saying that the money is not in their budget. They must demand the funds needed.

They have been given a sacred trust and must perform on behalf of the citizens of Los Angeles County. The same demands must be applied to city councils and state legislators and the governor.

Homeland Security has become one of the great union-busting projects of all time. And what about using Federal Troops to break strikes? That reminds us of Anastasio Somoza Garcia in Nicaragua.

In dictatorships, the legislative branch of government is a group of live rubber stamps. Does that sound familiar? American freedom and democracy cannot coexist with an imperial dictatorial presidency. Oh, yes. Dictatorships have prisons full of people. We now have 25% of the prisoners of the world and we only have 5% of the world's people.

In dictatorships, the actual power is the military and its interests. The President becomes a front for a police state. At this time, our military has over half of the budget of the US. Where your treasure is, there your heart will be.

Friends we are being destroyed by the virus of *militarism* and the clear indicator of that is the philosophy of *might makes right*. This is the only message I am getting from Mr. Bush.

So let's not talk about the ideology of fascism, let's talk about how dictatorial regimes conduct themselves. We are losing all the good things of the United States because of run away militarism. Any incompetent can start a war. It takes dialogue, collective genius and good will to maintain a polity of justice and peace.

Representative Nick Rahall

September 17, 2002

Today I would like to share with you excerpts from a message given to the Iraqi National Assembly by Congressman Nick Rahall, Member of the U.S. House of Representatives from West Virginia.

I come as an advocate of peace through dialogue. Instead of assuming that war must come, let us find ways to discover how to prove that war is unnecessary. A key to this terrible box that we're now locked in—is dialogue.

We are here to try and help open doors. Doors to genuine dialogue. It is time and, in my opinion, far past time that American and Iraqi officials talk to each other without threats. We want to open doors to possibilities that will protect life instead of maiming and killing. Doors that will give peace a chance.

We've had far too much heated rhetoric between our two countries. Another war in this region would be greatly damaging. Any new war would be a war against public health, and also against the environment.

Iraq is the cradle of civilization. We do not wish to see civilization strangled in its cradle. Iraq was once the Garden of Eden. Humanity must not turn the Garden of Eden into Hell.

The evidence from the last war is quite compelling:

- Degradation of the infrastructure;

- A wrecked economy;

- And, a shocking escalation of infant mortality, communicable diseases, and many other negative health indicators for the entire population.

We do not wish to see this devastation repeated.

In this context, I am reminded of what Dwight Eisenhower, the Great

U.S. general and President once said: "Every gun and rocket that is fired, every warship launched, signifies, in a final sense, a theft from those who hunger and are not fed, those who are cold and are not clothed.

The world in arms is not spending money alone. It is spending the sweat of its laborers, the genius of its scientists, the hopes of its children. But time is now terribly short to reverse the momentum toward war.

The Christian scriptures say "Blessed are the peacemakers." They do not say "Blessed are the warmongers." I happen to believe that the vast majority of the American people do not want to wage war, but would rather wage peace.

Our delegation is here on behalf of peace. We believe that a new war is not only unnecessary, but wrong.

Speaking personally, I will encourage my colleagues in the Congress to enter into dialogue with the Iraq National Assembly for the future benefit of both our nations.

Here ends excerpts from the talk of Congressman Nick Rahall to the Iraqi National Assembly.

Please direct your Congresspeople and your Senators to make similar delegations to Iraq before our fine young people are sent there to die.

War Mania

September 23, 2002

I just don't understand; when someone commits a singular murder, they are liable to receive the death penalty, and when our head of state plots the killing of countless civilians, we are supposed to recognize him as a statesman.

Indeed, organized crime is much more selective in its murders than our own government. Even organized crime generally plots the killing of one person at a time. Organized crime has rarely supported indiscriminate killing. Where is the moral compass here? Certainly not in government.

We are pleased that the Catholic Bishops of the United States have sent a letter to President Bush opposing any new war in Iraq. And congratulations on the three great ads placed in the New York Times and the Los Angeles Times this week by Americans Against the War in Iraq, Not in Our Name and the Office of the Americas.

Congratulations to Medea Benjamin and Diane Wilson for communicating with "War" Secretary Rumsfeld and trying to bring some rationality to his false, deceptive and murderous banter as he spoke to the House Armed Services Committee.

Friends, the "War" Secretary told lawmakers that Iraq poses the greatest threat to global stability. The statement is absolutely false. He forgot to mention the threat of his own country to global stability.

The war mania of Bush and Rumsfeld will manufacture a million new terrorists. This is what happens when people are unjustly oppressed. Take the case of Israel and Palestine. One side has an air force, one side has one of the strongest military forces in the world, one side has military bulldozers and has used all of these weapons against a people with no such armaments. The Palestinians began with street demonstrations and then continued with sling shots and now they are tragically engaged in suicide bombings.

This behavior is entirely predicable as people see their teenagers shot, as they have their homes destroyed because of the alleged crimes of their children. Instead of getting the message of history, our mindless leaders are imitating a failed policy.

Instead of learning from the contemporary disasters in Israel, Palestine and Afghanistan, we plan to repeat them on an ever-larger scale. Frankly, I don't think the planet is sustainable under our current militarists.

The administration tells us that war will liberate the Iraqi people. No, bombing Baghdad, a city of five million people, will not liberate them. It will kill them. And what is the motivation of the Bush people? One of this weeks three great national ads stated the following:

- War will take our minds off the bad economy

- War will distract us from the health care meltdown, the raids on Social Security, the assaults on the environment, the corporate scandals and the destruction of our civil liberties and unfortunately war frequently leads to the reelection of incumbents.

We must stop the war with Iraq before it starts. Historians will not forget the ineptitude and deceit of Rumsfeld who could state that Iraq looms as the world's gravest danger. In case you don't know it, Mr. Rumsfeld, Iraq is in ashes. It has been devastated by eleven years of endless bombing and a murderous embargo on its most vulnerable people. The real threat is from our chemical, biological and nuclear weapons not from Iraq. Everyone knows that if Iraq fired one such weapon it would be eliminated from the face of the earth.

What Mr. Rumsfeld has done here is insult the intelligence of every U.S. citizen. There is not one shred of truth in the statements he made to the Armed Services Committee. And to add insult to injury we have to observe the Democratic Senate Majority Leader Tom Daschle assure his cooperation with the Bush administration.

Let it not be said that the people in the United States did nothing when their government declared war without limit and instituted stark new measures of repression.

Israeli Solidarity

October 6, 2002

There seems to be a problem with heads of state. In country after country, the people are just beautiful and the heads of state are truly repulsive. This is certainly true of the unelected disaster in Washington today. And it is also true in England and Israel.

Nine Israeli women's peace groups have told Palestinians that they support their efforts to indict the Israeli Prime Minister, Ariel Sharon, for war crimes. The letter from the Coalition of Women for a Just Peace in Israel speaks of the suffering of the Palestinians and I quote:

> Our hearts ache to recall the terrible massacre that took place in the Sabra and Shatila refugee camps 20 years ago, which Israeli leaders allowed to take place. We condemn the brutal murders of your loved ones and we condemn the leaders who must be held accountable for these war crimes, Ariel Sharon above all.

The letter refers to some 1,700 Palestinians who were slaughtered in the massacre by Lebanese Militiamen allied to the Israelis. Israeli troops surrounded the camps as the killing went on but were told by their commanders not to interfere. Mr. Sharon was Israeli Minister of Defense at the time and was forced to resign after the Israeli Kahan commission condemned him and several senior Israeli officers for not preventing the slaughter. The letter also recalls how Palestinians were forced to flee their homes in 1948.

At the same time, Professor Avraham Oz at the University of Haifa expresses an urgent warning signed by a host of Israeli and international academics:

> We, members of Israeli academia, are horrified by the US buildup of aggression towards Iraq and by the Israeli political leadership's enthusiastic support for it. We are deeply worried by indications that the "fog

of war" could be exploited by the Israeli government to commit further crimes against the Palestinian people, up to full-fledged ethnic cleansing.

The Israeli ruling coalition includes parties that promote "transfer" of the Palestinian population as a solution to what they call "the demographic problem." Politicians are regularly quoted in the media as suggesting forcible expulsion . . . Chief of Staff Moshe Ya'alon described the Palestinians as a "cancerous manifestation" and equated the military actions in the Occupied Territories with "chemotherapy," suggesting that more radical "treatment" may be necessary. Prime Minister Sharon has backed what he calls this "assessment of reality." Escalating racist demagoguery concerning the Palestinian citizens of Israel may indicate the scope of the crimes that are possibly being contemplated.

We call upon the International Community to pay close attention to events that unfold within Israel and in the Occupied Territories, to make it absolutely clear that crimes against humanity will not be tolerated, and to take concrete measures to prevent such crimes from taking place.

It seems that in the United States and in Israel, the population is simply saying to the heads of state: "We are better than that."

After some more relevant music we are privileged to have a guest from Israel, Aliyah Strauss.

Bio for Aliyah Strauss:

In 1985 she became active in Bridge for Peace and Co-existence, a group of Jews and Arabs who met regularly to discuss issues of common interest. Since 1990, she has been a leader of Women in Black, a women's peace organization. She is active in numerous women's and peace organizations, such as the Coalition for Women for Peace and Bat Shalom. In 1997, she was elected as the President of the Israel section of the Women's International League for Peace and Freedom (WILPF).

She has committed her life to achieving peace in the Middle East. The principles the organizations she belongs to agree on the following:

- An end to the occupation

- Establishment of a Palestinian state, side by side with the state of Israel, based on the 1967 borders

- Recognition of Jerusalem as the shared capital of the two states

- Opposition to militarism that permeates Israeli society

- Equality, inclusion and justice for Palestinian citizens of Israel

- Full involvement of women in negotiations for peace

- Social and economic justice for Israel's citizens and integration of Israel in the Middle East region

Thanks so much, Aliyah Strauss. Wishing you much success with your work for peace and justice between Palestine and Israel.

Cult Madness

October 7, 2002

The holocaust in Iraq continues. It was not enough to drop 88,000 tons of bombs in 1991. It was not enough to continue the bombing for eleven more years. It was not enough to embargo food and medicine, to starve the people and watch their children die of malnutrition and preventable disease.

Many of us have been to Iraq and we can assure you that the country is now in ashes. Nearly two million people have died in this holocaust and the cult leaders in Washington have determined that we must kill more. As they kill and maim millions, they talk as if there is one person living in Iraq. And that is part of the cult madness.

This war is being planned against the wishes of the sovereign people of the United States. The presidency is at the lowest ebb in our history. An unelected president of the United States is acting to the detriment of the people of the United States, so the head of state in Israel is acting to the detriment of the Israeli people.

These two cult leaders are telling their constituents to commit suicide. And many members of the cult are in compliance. What does Sharon expect to accomplish with his 200 nuclear weapons, world peace? Peace in Israel? The era of the Good Neighbor? He will accomplish none of this. On the contrary he and Mr. Bush have the potential to initiate a nuclear World War with the policy of preemptive first strikes. They will only accomplish the peace of the cemetery. The terror with which they behave will and is blowing back at them. But not only at them but to the beautiful people who live in the United States and Israel.

China can follow the deadly logic and attack Taiwan. India can follow the cult and strike Pakistan. Russia can eliminate Chechnya. And we all can spend our few remaining hours in nuclear winter. And what do we see in our Democratic Congresspeople? Many of them have joined the cult of necrophilia as well. We want our congresspeople to know that they are either with us or they are fired. Pay attention, Mr. Waxman.

Friends, we are not here to curse the darkness, but we are here to identify a national cult that is about to take more lives than the Third Reich ever did. We must stop this holocaust. A defunct Democratic Party and the war-mongering Republicans have given us no choice but to protest in the streets. The commercial media has done everything possible to silence and censor our movement. And friends, maybe that is a good thing because we are now in every city and state of the United States as well as Israel. We will build a peace system. We will abolish the war system.

Join us in San Francisco and in Washington on October 26th. And join The School of the Americas at Fort Benning, Georgia in November.

Calls in to Congress are numbering up to 1000 to one against this war. We are being ignored, the will of the people is being disregarded.

We did not give you our hard earned money to buy cluster bombs for the children of Iraq. We did not authorize you to conduct a holocaust in our name.

Not in Our Name

> *We believe that as people living in the United States*
> *It is our responsibility to resist the injustices*
> *Done by our government, in our names.*
> *Not in our name will you wage endless war.*
> *There can be no more deaths, no more transfusions of blood for oil.*
> *We pledge to make common cause with the people of the world to*
> *bring about justice,*
> *freedom and peace . . .*
> *Another world is possible*
> *And we pledge to make it real.*

International Murder, Incorporated

October 14, 2002

We have just experienced an inductive study of how we are not represented. Calls to every Congressional Office have come in from 25 to 1
up to 1000 to 1 against the pending war in Iraq. But what difference
should that make, it's only the will of the sovereign people of the United
States who are demanding peace. Since when did they count? Since
when did they matter?

Friends, what we are witnessing is the final takeover of the United
States by the Military, Industrial, Prison and Gun Complex. They don't
care what you want. Your representatives do not represent, they do not
dissent, they do not oppose. They are indistinguishable from the rubber
stamps of any tin pot dictatorship. In order to stay in power they are not
willing to exercise the power they have.

You have witnessed a cynical disregard for the Constitution of the
United States. Mr. Bush has no constitutional power to declare war anywhere but, if this precedent continues, he will illegally be given power
to declare war everywhere. The Supreme Court, however, has the power
to declare this congressional resolution unconstitutional which it must
do. Aside from the national crime of disregarding the Constitution, Mr.
Bush is committing an international crime against peace by his endless
threats of preemptive strikes.

Planned assassination is also an international crime against peace.
Mr. Bush is now solely in charge of International Murder, Incorporated.
Congress people . . . wouldn't it be better to go back to your used car lot
with self respect and confidence that you did the right thing? Wouldn't
it be better to go back to your law firm with some integrity rather than to
remain a prostitute for mass murder?

Each and every one of the congressional corporate lackeys who voted
for the war resolution must be replaced. They have betrayed their sacred
trust, they have betrayed their oath of office, they have betrayed the people
of the United States and they have betrayed the Constitution.

Perhaps it is fortunate that they approved of this massacre before election time. Now it is up to us to give them an electoral response of no confidence, no respect, and no future. Quite simply, they are either with us or they are fired.

They are marching in a trance with a serial killer who walked through Texas signing death warrants for the mentally ill and the poorly represented, leading to one of the largest frenzies of cold blooded state sponsored killings in our history.

And now, the fear merchant continues to sell his wares. Bush has become a master of the Ghost Story and tales of horror. His eyes flash back and forth and he tells lies about a destroyed nation.

George Bush forgot to talk about the danger of *our* weapons of mass destruction. George forgot to talk about our chemical and biological warfare capability. And he forgot to talk about the extreme danger of accident with these weapons of mass destruction. He also forgot to talk about how his bloodthirsty policy will manufacture more terrorists.

We don't wonder about whether Pakistan, India, Israel and China have nuclear weapons of mass destruction. We know they do. The madness of our attack on Iraq will give these states the go-ahead for their own first strike actions.

Christian Fundamentalism

October 21, 2002

Friends, we have a pathetic situation in which the sharing of delusional ideas by two unlikely sources may be the actual spark of an international conflagration. I'm speaking of the very strange relationship between fundamentalist Christians and the Likud Party of Israel. Groups of Christians, who focus on Armageddon and the Rapture and stupidly translating this as the need for a war between Muslims and Jews to bring about the Second Coming of Christ, are capable of transforming the Israel/Palestine conflict into a war of civilizations that will be worldwide. Young George Bush is in the loop of this anti-intellectual, ahistorical and fanatical trap.

As the United States directs its attention to Islamic Fundamentalism, it refuses to see the Taliban-like elements of Christian and Jewish fundamentalism. As we wage war on Islam at home and abroad, we continue to support extremist settlers in the occupied territories of Israel. While Muslim charities are shut down in the United States without the government offering any evidence of links to terrorists, known terrorist organizations such as the Jewish Defense League are not placed on the government's list of terrorist organizations.

Ralph Reed, Pat Robertson, Jerry Falwell and other fundamentalist leaders are now supporting the most extreme Israeli positions. They claim they are hastening the Second Coming of Christ.

Biblical literalists generally seem to miss the entire point of scriptural language and this case is no exception. They have dug up dispensational premillennialism, the theology of John Darby in the 19th century as reflected in the works of Hal Linsay's, *The Late Great Planet Earth* or the *Left Behind* books by the Rev. Tim LaHaye and Jerry B. Jenkins. They claim that Christ's faithful will be caught up in the clouds and given new, immortal bodies while the rest of the population faces the horrors of the last days.

All of this requires that the Jewish Temple destroyed in 70 AD be rebuilt and after a period of tribulation Jesus will return. Jews who accept

65

Jesus will enter the Kingdom along with faithful Christians . . . others will perish violently.

The fundamentalist Jews, however, claim this will be the establishment of the state of Israel and the extension of its sovereignty to the West Bank, Gaza and beyond. The Temple will be rebuilt, the Messiah will arrive and the redemption of the world will be at hand.

Rabbi Haim Dov Beliak states of the fundamentalist settlers: "They are very problematic because they are going to cause World War III. There's a complete denial of any rights that the Arabs might have. There's an attempt to use the Bible as a land deed . . . it's fantastic the length of religious nationalistic jingoism these people are prepared to go," said Beliak.

There is no distinction between the settler movement and the current Israeli Government. Sharon is the architect of the settler movement and the creator of the idea that there is no room for Arabs to live between the Jordan River and the Mediterranean Sea.

There is simply no support for these fanatical fundamentalist interpretations in reputable Catholic or mainline Protestant theological perspectives. It seems to me that there is only one fundamentalism wearing different costumes. It is simply the psychological fixation that, "I have the truth and outside my truth there are only devils. What is more, I have to kill the devil."

Preemptive Nonviolence

October 28, 2002

Congratulations on the victorious demonstrations throughout the United States. Congratulations are due because after a year of disinformation, war mongering, fear mongering, lies, deceit and threats, these were the largest demonstrations since the destruction of Vietnam.

And these demonstrations were prior to the war. They were preemptive non-violent messages given by 80,000 of us in San Francisco and 200,000 in the nation's capital as reported by CNN.

The struggle itself is the victory. *La lucha misma es la victoria!* We pledged in San Francisco to be wise as serpents and simple as doves. We choose to select instruments of change that are both militant and non-violent. San Francisco has a history of utilizing the General Strike, this is one of the ways it became a strong labor union city. We are also evaluating the general strike as another powerful weapon against those who would betray the people of the United States by their treacherous support for an absolutely unnecessary and genocidal war.

The greatest myth in our culture today is that of powerlessness. We are not powerless. We are powerful. We will continue to show our power in disciplined, militant and peaceful mobilization in solidarity with oppressed people.

Our unelected head of state is a disgrace to the world. He can talk about nothing except the massacre of Iraqi people, Iraqi children. He and his father have presided over a holocaust of 1.7 million Iraqi people as they talk about assassinating one man. There are no elements of organized crime that have been so sloppy in their work. Medical clinics across our nation are closing to pay for planet busting weapons of mass destruction while we pick at the bones of the corpses of Iraq to pretend to find weapons that they do not have. This is a theft from our homeless people, our tens of millions with no health care, our disintegrating schools and our toxic culture of necrophilia that is love of death!

We must dare to change the course of history. We are not here to watch history; we are here to participate in the making of history. We will change history by continuing with creative, mass mobilizations all over the United States. We are a sovereign people. We will continue with the weapons of non-violence, we will speak at the ballot box to remove from office any members of Congress who betrayed the people by supporting the Bush War Resolution.

Congratulations Paul Wellstone. We are proud of you. And if every member of the House and Senate would follow your example, they too could meet their Maker as proud, as you must be saying that they had fought the good fight for the people, they had finished the course for democracy, they had been victorious in the struggle for justice and peace instead of selling their birth-right for a stinking bowl of petroleum.

Practice Bombing

November 4, 2002

Policies of empire are expanding on a daily basis. The carrier USS Abraham Lincoln has arrived in the Persian Gulf and Donald H. Rumsfeld has illegally given U.S. warplanes the go-ahead to attack ever broader sectors of the Iraqi people. More areas are being bombed now than in the lawless attacks of the past eleven years. This is being done with a combination of practice bombing and real bombing. Both are crass terrorism.

Practice bombing puts people in the same situation as mock assassination. A combination of practice bombing and actual bombing both terrorizes and kills. Because a carrier is considered sovereign U.S. territory, political considerations of opposition from the surrounding countries have been ignored.

Let's consider turn about as fair play. Suppose China was practice bombing off of Point Magu, and suppose that some of the time they were actually dropping real bombs on Malibu and vicinity. How would we respond? Would we flippantly say, "Hey, we don't mind the practice bombing so much but what really irks us is if we lock our radar on your attacking planes, then the bombing runs become real."

Then China might say, "Be a good sport, you should let us continue these exercises and by the way, it is certainly fair for us to bomb you if you lock your radar onto our incoming aircraft. Do you think we want our very expensive planes or even our pilots to be harmed? Why do you insist on interfering with our legitimate maneuvers?

How did we become so numb to the behavior of our military? This appears to be the sacralization of imperial behavior. Toleration of this kind of behavior represents nationalistic fundamentalism. And now, even more aircraft carriers are on the way to the Persian Gulf to expand this combined mission of practice bombing and actual bombing. Let's take a look at history.

On August 27, 1992 The United States together with France and Britain imposed a no-fly zone on Iraq, forbidding Iraqi planes to fly south of the 32nd parallel. The U.S. claims it was protecting Shiites from Saddam Hussein. But actually the heaviest U.S. bombing in the Gulf War occurred in the south of Iraq in the very area which is now a no-fly zone.

Neither this demarcation at the 32nd parallel nor the previous imposition of a no-fly zone north of the 36th parallel was part of the UN cease fire agreement, nor was this sanctioned by any UN resolution. These violations of Iraq's sovereignty broke the country into three parts, leaving the US in control of the areas with the richest oil reserves.

No Child Left Behind Act

November 11, 2002

I recently visited the Valley Alternative School to talk about peace together with a group of Vietnam Veterans. The high school seniors were eager to hear about Washington's War Mania.

In preparation for this visit, I was reading about the No Child Left Behind Act, a sweeping education law passed earlier this year. It is 670 pages long and it includes a requirement for public secondary schools to provide military recruiters not only access to their facilities but also with contact information for every student.

This means that when the principal of a high school receives a letter from military recruiters demanding a list of all students including names addresses and phone numbers the school officials are expected to comply. And what if they don't? They face a cut-off of all federal aid. Never mind that this is a violation of the current student privacy laws. Unfortunately recruiters do not tell the truth. They speak of education, travel and good times. But they fail to make it clear that when you get into the service you will do what you are told or go to military prison. One of the veterans said he had 73 troops under his direction. He said they had all been told of educational opportunities in the service and that exactly three of them received any educational opportunity in the service.

It seems that the lies begin in Kindergarten. Students are told that George Washington could not tell a lie. The story is a falsehood concocted by a Reverend who wanted to teach children not to lie.

Education, so-called, is very disrespectful of the intelligence of children. Kindergarten children could easily discuss the merits of war and peace. They should be taught about the holocausts imposed on the indigenous, the slaves and the Armenians, the Jews, the Vietnamese, the Central Americans and the Iraqis in their earliest years of grade school.

I felt a great sadness as I reflected on the fact that student alumni of this high school went off to die as the enemy in places where they were not wanted. They did not know the issues, they did not know the history, they did know the motivation for the very war in which they died. They were condemned to repeat history because they had not studied it.

There are now over 500,000 high school students in the Junior ROTC nationwide. Funds are taken from the budget of the Los Angeles Unified School District to pay for this military training. Non-credentialed trainers are teaching the students to aim, shoot and kill at the very time we are trying to get the guns out of our schools. One third of the homeless people in Los Angeles are veterans, the government's historic rejection of veterans is traceable from the Revolution of 1776 to the Gulf War. A substantial percentage of the veterans of the Gulf War are suffering from the effects of depleted uranium, chemical warfare and medical experimentation. They are victims of our own friendly fire.

Cluster Bombing

November 19, 2002

All the pieces are now in place in Iraq. The cluster bombs are ready to drop on civilians. Children are especially attracted to cluster bombs. I am speaking of CBU-87. It is seven feet, six inches long. It weighs 950 pounds and it contains 200 bomblets.

The bomblets are called BLU-97. They are 6.7 inches long and they weigh 3.3 pounds each. They each have 10 ounces of Cyclotol Zirconium and on detonation each bomblet fractures into about 300 steel fragments, covering an area the size of a football field. Cluster bombs have been used in Yugoslavia, Kosovo, Vietnam, Cambodia, Laos, Sudan, Lebanon, Ethiopia, Chechnya, the Falkands, the Persian Gulf and Afghanistan.

Aside from the indescriminate murder caused by these bombs, about ten percent of them do not detonate. The bright yellow unexploded bombs make an attractive toys for children to play with and to lose their lives. Also the unexploded yellow bomblets are often confused with similar colored food packages as were dropped from U.S. planes in Afghanistan. Human Rights Watch reported that U.S. planes dropped 1,150 cluster bombs on 188 locations in Afghanistan.

Just think of how civilization has deteriorated from the days of the Aztecs and the Mayas. They did not kill in battle, they just used a few captives for human sacrifice. Just think how civilization has deteriorated from the days of cannibalism. Cannibal cultures only used what they could eat. We have deteriorated to the point where the killing machines exist simply to kill.

Oh, the glory of modern warfare! And friends, just think of our motivation for blowing the heads off of Iraqi children. The motivation is to have higher prices for gasoline in the United States. Why do we say that?

Well, it is quite simple. If we purchased oil from the nationalized system in Iraq it would be far cheaper than purchasing it from corporations which will be granted the ownership of Iraqi oil after our annihilation of their people and their culture.

Currently gasoline is five cents a gallon in Iraq. Water is twenty-five cents a gallon. That's right. The effect of spending our treasury and our finest young people to die in Iraq will simply be higher prices for gasoline in the United States. So when the body bags start coming home remember that our children died for higher oil prices.

Part of the terror of this unnecessary and immoral war is the inability of the world's richest nation to offer health care, a living wage or housing to its working people. Congratulations are due to the historic preemptive peace movement that is now blossoming throughout the world.

It is a source of joy to us to observe that millions of intelligent and peace loving people are simply not willing to conduct mass murder in Iraq to obtain a net increase in the price of fuel at home.

Oakland School District Teach-in

November 25, 2002

Here is some very good news from Adele Siegel and her Peace Guides. Students in kindergarten through 12th grade learned about the proposed war in Iraq at a teach-in sponsored by the Oakland School District. Fifth-graders from Sequoia Elementary School spoke in favor of the teach-in at Wednesday's board meeting and read letters they had written to Bush opposing an Iraq war.

"When you go to war, you are setting a bad example for all the kids in the U.S.A.," one letter stated. "Wars and fights are not right, and bombing beautiful things is not right either."

The students invited Bush to come to a weekly class at Sequoia that teaches youngsters how to resolve problems without fighting. "It's not fair for other people (if) they get killed, because they haven't done anything to George Bush, Bush is only mad at one person (Iraqi President Saddam Hussein)," Jennifer said. "We think (Bush) should come to our class on Wednesday to learn some (conflict resolution) skills."

The fifth-graders showed they understood that the United States once supported Iraq militarily. "We think it's strange to go to war with a country you taught war to," student Emma Styles-Swaim said. "We think it's strange because, well, it's weird."

And here is the resolution:

Resolution Calling for a Day of Public Education on War Against Iraq

WHEREAS, the United States government states that it is preparing to initiate a war against the nation of Iraq; and WHEREAS, an attack on Iraq by the United States would have enormous human, financial and political consequences in the United States and the world community; and WHEREAS, it is essential that the people of the United States be well-informed on the causes and consequences of military action by their government, THEREFORE BE IT RESOLVED, that the Board of Education of the Oakland Unified School District decrees that there shall be city-wide public education at the school level concerning the background of the current crisis concerning Iraq, the options available to the United States government for attempting to resolve that crisis, and the likely consequences of a United States military attack on Iraq; FURTHER, that the District's Division of Student Achievement shall work with the Oakland Education Association to develop a list of available resources and lessons that are appropriate for the classroom; FURTHER, that schools may invite parents and other members of the public to participate in the educational programs; and FURTHER, that no student or teacher who objects to participation in such educational programs shall be required to do so.

Friends, we must demand that the Los Angeles Unified School District and every other school district carry out this resolution. Call Caprice Young, the President of the LAUSD, and insist that our board follow the example of Oakland.

Voices in the Wilderness

December 2, 2002

This week I spoke with Kathy Kelly in Baghdad. She is the founder of Voices in the Wilderness. She and her associates have gone to Iraq many times. But now, with the upcoming holocaust, some of her volunteers have decided to stay in Iraq for the duration. Many others will be present there for a week or two on delegations.

These volunteers do not go to Iraq to commit suicide. They do not go there for media glory. Indeed the media is afraid of them. Their story will be told for centuries but the media prefers to talk about celebrity gossip.

Voices in the Wilderness are the voices of witness, voices that all can hear if they will but listen, if they are not deaf to reality.

Members of Voices in the Wilderness await the bombs as they reside in the very target areas to be attacked. Their voices cry out for the voiceless of Iraq, the voiceless in Palestine. The voiceless of our homeless and our forgotten children. With the prophet Micah they love peace, do justice and walk humbly with their God. They are from a variety of religions and non-religions. Their voices transcend all sectarianism. They give the lie to the war mongers who long to create a war between Islam and Christianity or between any other combination of religions. Such religious militarists have not had a new idea since the days of the Crusades.

Voices in the Wilderness knows that the name of one's religion is actually meaningless. One can profess any religion by name and be a devil or a saint. The name of the religion is irrelevant. The only valid gauge of spirituality is conduct.

Conduct which reflects justice, peace, joy, love endurance, patience and compassion is the fruit of valid spirituality. Anything else is a sham. This is what led John Lennon to say, "Imagine no religion." If religion does not promote the fruits of the Spirit, it would be better to imagine no religion.

The international movement for justice and peace has more spirituality than any religion that attempts to bless war. War is not to be blessed. War is to be abolished along with the slavery and servitude which it demands.

Thanks voices in the wilderness.

Not everyone is expected to go to Iraq and everyone does not have to; but everyone can do something. Workers who stuff envelopes and send out emails are messengers of peace. Putting 500,000 people on the streets of Washington DC on Saturday, January 18, 2003 will be done by messengers of peace.

The 30 or so wars now taking place in the name of religion have no authentic spiritual substance. They are fraudulent. They are simply political conflicts using religion as a cloak for malice.

Now do we understand why John Lennon said, "Imagine no religion?" Keep your roots, keep your religion but don't let it be used to oppress innocent people. Religion must not bless war.

Peace on Earth! No War on Iraq!

December 10. 2002

We celebrate the life of Phil Berrigan with so many memories. He reminded us of Isaiah, Jeremiah or John the Baptist. In 1968, thirteen of us sat in a basement at 1620 "S" Street in Washington, D.C. as he presented a plan to napalm the draft files at Catonsville, Maryland. The question for the people of the United States: "Is it better to burn paper or people?" Nine of the thirteen entered into the action. Many of us were present at that famous trial with William Kuntzler, Bishop Pike, Dorothy Day and so many other peace makers. We went on to form the Berrigan Defense Committee on the West Coast. This draft file burning action was imitated about one hundred times in the United States. A good deal of paper was incinerated. We are not aware of any injury to any person in this wave of "non-violent civil" disobedience.

We can't afford the luxury of many such reminiscences, however, the present moment is even more challenging. *Phil Berrigan, Presente*! You stand out as a beacon of light in a very dark hour and you will be remembered long after the current gallery of psychotic war mongers is rightfully forgotten.

And now we stand at the verge of an unnecessary, illegal, immoral slaughter. We must rise to the occasion in resistance. We were betrayed by our Congress as they gave in to the powers of corporate greed.

Once again, we must take to the streets in massive numbers. We will join hundreds of thousands in Washington, D.C. on January 18, 2003. This is the Martin Luther King Weekend and we will honor him as we recall his words at Riverside Church on April 4, 1967: "The greatest purveyor of violence in the world today is my own government."

On January 19, the Grassroots Peace Congress will be convened in Washington, D.C. As we oppose this criminal war in the Middle East we will demand that our hard earned tax money be used for education, healthcare, housing and human needs rather than mass murder.

A final quote from Phil Berrigan: "War on terrorism by the U.S. is impossible. We are the number one terrorist."

79

Christmas Then and Now

December 16, 2002

Now at this time, Caesar Augustus issued a decree for a census of the whole world to be taken. This census, the first, took place while Quirinius was governor of Syria, and everyone went to their own town to be registered. So Joseph set out from the town of Nazareth in Galilee and traveled up to Judea, to the town of David called Bethlehem, since he was of David's House and line, in order to be registered together with Mary his betrothed, who was with child.

And so this very day in Los Angeles, people from afar have been ordered to register and this is the last chance for many who will be considered criminals if they don't register (and if they do register they may be taken away in handcuffs and possibly disappear).

On with the story.

> Then the wise men arrived and Herod was furious when he realized that he had been outwitted by them, and in Bethlehem and its surrounding districts he had all the male children killed who were two years old or under . . .

And Bethlehem remains as an occupied city today. Then the little family had to escape into Egypt by night. This is the plight of refugees the world over. They are hated because they are different. They are exploited because they cannot communicate and they are considered second and third class members of society to be used, abused and discarded.

Well, the family stayed in Egypt until the King was dead. They went back to the land of Israel and when Joseph learned that Archelaus had succeeded his father Herod as ruler of Judea he decided to go to Galilee and he settled in the town of Nazareth.

So the child was brought up in Nazareth and as a young adult he went into the Synagogue on the Sabbath and stood up to read. They handed him the scroll of the prophet Isaiah and he read:

The spirit of the Lord has been given to me, for he has anointed me. He has sent me to bring the good news to the poor, to proclaim liberty to captives and to the blind new sight, to set the downtrodden free, to proclaim the Lord's year of favor.

He said, "This text is being fulfilled today even as you listen." And he won the approval of all.

The scene then changed rapidly when Jesus explained that his message was universal, not parochial. He said:

There were many widows in Israel, I can assure you, in Elijah's day, when heaven remained shut for three years and six months and a great famine raged throughout the land, but Elijah was not sent to any one of these: he was sent to a widow at Zarephath, a Sidonian town. And in the prophet Elisha's time there were many lepers in Israel, but not one of these was cured, except the Syrian, Naaman.

This message is universal. It is not sectarian, it is not nationalistic, it is not for one ethnic group, it for the one race that lives on the planet, it is for the human race and it incorporates every spiritual path.

Lori Berenson

December 23, 2002

In a letter to her mother, Lori Berenson made an observation regarding a baby visiting her prison wing being rocked to sleep in a lawn chair:

> When Micaela gets hysterical, you just put her in the lawn chair and move it and she's thrilled. My theory is that if the NASA folks could create a giant lawn chair to cradle the planet perhaps we could attain world peace. It's such a miraculous solution!

And here is Lori's holiday message from Huacariz Prison in Cajamarca, Peru:

Dear Friends,

I very much thank you for your concern and support over the years. In this holiday season and with the coming of the new year, a point of reflection for all should include what we can do to make the world a better place, with less war, less hate, and fewer excuses for killing in the name of wealth, power, or greed—which is just so wrong.

My personal reflection, which has grown over these years in jail, is that if we all don't work to humanize this world I don't know how we'll end up, and I believe we owe it to the future generations to leave them a better world to live in.

In this light I will close, wishing you the best in this holiday season and hoping for a good new year.

Sincerely,

Lori Berenson

Lori's parents, Mark and Rhoda add this message:

We join Lori in thanking you for all the support you have given her and us. Lori has now completed her seventh year wrongfully imprisoned in Peru and she still remains true to her beliefs in social justice and human rights.

As you know, the Inter-American Commission has brought the case in defense of its position favoring Lori to the Inter-American Court of Human Rights in San Jose, Costa Rica. In September, the Court agreed to hold hearings. We are concerned, however, that this process could take two or more years while Lori suffers in prison for no reason. We are also concerned that Peru might not comply with the Court decision - even though as a member of the Inter-American Court system it has agreed to abide by Court decisions.

In the new year we will once again be urging President Bush, Secretary of State Powell, and members of Congress to persuade the Peruvian government to release Lori as soon as possible.

We thank each of you for supporting our efforts, either financially or with letters, phone-calls and/or actions. Contributions to the Committee to Free Lori Berenson have helped us to maintain the office in Washington, travel to Peru to visit Lori, and continue the fight for her freedom. We hope you can help us continue in this struggle.

Growth of the Peace Movement

December 29, 2002

I'm in Albany today and we are looking at a new reality. Albany's *Times Union* has a front page story on the emerging peace movement in this region. Veterans for Peace are given a half page photo and the *Los Angeles Times* is quoted as saying that 72% of the people don't see sufficient reason for war.

The peace movement against war on Iraq is at a higher level nationally than it was at the end of the war in Vietnam. We are now part of the largest preemptive peace movement in history.

Our war mongering leadership has contributed to the success of the peace movement. I teach Logic and I don't see any logic coming out of Washington, D.C. Here is a statement from Mr. Rumsfeld:

> Anyone who knows anything isn't talking, and anyone with any sense isn't talking. Therefore the people that are talking to the media are by definition people who don't know anything. (*Los Angeles Times*)

Rumsfeld thinks he can fight two wars at once; Korea, Iraq, and what about three wars or four wars. Don't forget Iran, Libya, Syria, Palestine, Indonesia, Pakistan, the Philippines, New Jersey . . . China?

It seems to me that our leadership has become sociopathic, and this also contributes to the success of the peace movement. Our grossly excessive list of weapons of mass destruction and mass terror has thinking people worried. As a social scientist, I would say that the social psychosis in which we are living is a bi-product of necrophilia or love of death.

Our leadership is breathing threats of slaughter to the whole world. We have arrived at the point where the CIA has to tell the Administration that if it carries out its bloody agenda there will be an increase of terror at home.

Here is a case where the leadership of Mr. Bush is recklessly endangering the people of the United States. And think about it, we are supposed to pay for this disaster! The money that should have gone to health care delivery has gone to pay for a lemon called the B-2 bomber at only one billion a copy. Funds that should have gone to education have gone to illegally develop new nuclear weapons of mass destruction.

Depleted uranium has depleted the health of Iraqis and Serbians. Depleted uranium has also depleted our troops who came home from the first Iraq War with Gulf War Illness.

"Each weapon that is made represents a theft from the poor." Thank you President Eisenhower. Indeed militarism is a theft from our common good, our common wealth. The entire public sector of the United States is depleted. Unemployment insurance is running out. Medicare payments to doctors are being cut (many doctors did not even accept the previous payments).

Remember your history. The peace movement was correct when we said that Laos was being bombed. The President denied it . . . and he ultimately resigned. Remember when we said millions of people, mainly civilians were being killed. History has borne this out; some three million people were killed in the holocaust of Vietnam.

We are not talking about war for freedom or liberation, we are talking about wars of aggression, imperial wars. The military of the world at peace is the greatest threat to the environment. The toxicity of the military is damaging the planet. And what our pathetic rogues gallery of 19th century war mongers does not seem to understand is that the planet cannot be sustained if the world's military is at war.

Any attack on Iraq or Korea is a threat to the planet. Any such wars gives the go-ahead for India (which is led by the equivalent of the KKK) to attack Pakistan, or for China to attack Taiwan, or for Israel to attack Palestine.

Indeed, our hubris is killing us. Each and every Greek drama identifies the arrogance of power to be the downfall of the person and the nation. And so it is today. Our leadership is toying not only with the destruction of Iraq but with the destruction of the United States of America.

We must not let this happen and so we continue with a nationwide and worldwide peace movement.

Harold Pinter

January 9, 2003

Here are some thoughts from Harold Pinter, one of the world's greatest living playwrights. He is speaking to the House of Commons in the United Kingdom, and he says:

> There's an old story about Oliver Cromwell. After he had taken the town of Drogheda the citizens were brought to the main square. Cromwell announced to his Lieutenants: "Kill all the women and rape all the men." One of his aides said: "Excuse me General. Isn't it the other way around?" A voice from the crowd called out: "Mr. Cromwell knows what he's doing!"
>
> That voice is the voice of Tony Blair "Mr. Bush knows what he's doing!" But the fact is that Mr. Bush and his gang do know what they're doing and Blair, also knows what they're doing. They are determined, quite simply, to control the world and the world's resources. And they don't give a damn how many people they murder on the way. And Blair goes along with it.
>
> He hasn't the support of the Labor Party, he hasn't the support of the country or of the celebrated "international community." How can he justify taking this country into a war nobody wants? The very idea that he has any influence over Bush is laughable. His supine acceptance of American bullying is pathetic.
>
> As for the American elephant, it has grown to be a monster of grotesque and obscene proportions. The "special relationship" between the USA and the United Kingdom has, in the last twelve years, brought about the deaths of thousands upon thousands of people in Iraq, Afghanistan and Serbia. All this in pursuit of the American and British "moral crusade," to bring "peace and stability to the world."
>
> The use of depleted uranium in the Gulf War has been particularly effective. Radiation levels in Iraq are appallingly high. Babies are born with no brain, no eyes, no genitals. Where they do have ears, mouths or rectums, all that issues from these orifices is blood. Blair and Bush are of course totally indifferent to such facts, not forgetting the charming,

grinning, beguiling Bill Clinton, who was apparently given a standing ovation at the Labor Party Conference. For what? Killing Iraqi children? Or Serbian children?

Bush has said: "We will not allow the worlds worst weapons to remain in the hands of the worlds worst leaders." Quite right. Look in the mirror chum. That's you. The US is at this moment developing advanced systems of "weapons of mass destruction" and is prepared to use them where it sees fit. It has walked away from international agreements on biological and chemical weapons, refusing to allow any inspection of its own factories. It is holding hundreds of Afghans prisoner in Guantanamo Bay, allowing them no legal redress, although they are charged with nothing, holding them captive virtually forever.

It is insisting on immunity from the international criminal court, a stance which beggars believe but which is now supported by Great Britain. The hypocrisy is breathtaking. Tony Blair's contemptible subservience to this criminal American regime demeans and dishonors this country.

Thus ends Harold Pinter's comments to the House of Commons.

Los Angeles Peace Mobilization

January 11, 2003

Congratulations on being part of the greatest preemptive peace movement in history! *La lucha misma es la Victoria*. The struggle itself is the victory. We must confront our contradictory government.

The head of state is contradictory to the hopes, desires and anxieties of the people of the United States. The presidential appointments are contradictory to the common good of the commonwealth.

If they are assigned to protect the environment, they are enemies of the environment. If they are assigned to protect the rights of labor, they are enemies of labor. If they are assigned to housing, they are opposed to housing. If they are assigned to health care, they support the ill health of tens of millions of our citizens. If they are assigned to defense, they are the world's most avaricious warmongers.

They have destroyed the nation of Iraq by twelve years of endless bombing, by calculated starvation, by calculated restriction of medicine by endless lies and misinformation.

The current head of state is an imposter who was never elected. He has approved a policy of summary assassination and torture.

And now under the darkness of an ever greater holocaust in Iraq, he continues to ignore the bloody occupation of Palestine.

We are blessed this week to have the presence of Adam Shapiro and his wife. As leaders of the International Solidarity Movement, they invite us to join the internationals in Palestine who have proven to be a restraint on the occupying forces. Similarly, Kathy Kelly invites us to join Voices in the Wilderness now stationed as witnesses in Iraq. The forces of our moral revolution will be victorious.

Militarism is destroying the United States of America. Militarism is destroying Israel. Militarism will destroy this little planet now gasping for breath.

We do not want to mimic the forces of militarism by second-class violence. We have seen enough of that with the second-class Republicans who call themselves Democrats.

Mark "No War" on every dollar bill, on every five dollar bill and every piece of currency of any amount.

And as for our future, we will go on to Washington and San Francisco this week. And what of Los Angeles? I propose that we conduct daily vigils here at this Federal Building and the West Side Federal Building . . .

We have four major groups here. Two groups can take responsibility for each of the buildings. Let us divide up the labor, let us divide up the days of the vigil and let us be present to remind this rouge state that we do not intend to pay for this war with our money, nor with our time, nor with the lives of our youth who are endlessly recruited from our high schools.

Congratulations on your non-violence and congratulations on your struggle to build an international system of justice and peace.

Hasta la Victoria de justicia y paz, siempre.

The War Machine

January 23, 2003

These are the words of Supreme Court Justice Robert L. Jackson, Chief US Prosecutor at the Nuremberg Tribunal, August 12, 1945:

> We must make clear to the Germans that the wrong for which their fallen leaders are on trial is not that they lost the war, but that they started it. And we must not allow ourselves to be drawn into a trial of the causes of the war, for our position is that no grievances or policies will justify resort to aggressive war. It is utterly renounced and condemned as an instrument of policy.

And in support of Justice Jackson, Dr. Andreas Toupadakis, who served as a scientist at Los Alamos and Lawrence Livermore reminds us of the erroneous thinking that surrounds our contemporary war mania.

What is lately often heard are phrases like: "We would support a US-led unilateral strike on Iraq only with UN endorsement." Or, "We would support a unilateral invasion if clear evidence emerged that Iraq had weapons of mass destruction." Or, "There should not be a war with Iraq because there is no proof that Iraq was involved with the 9/11 terrorist attack." And the list goes on.

But all these people with good intention fail to see the lethal trap before their eyes. If the war machine has decided to wage another aggressive war against another nation, it will sooner or later find a reason to justify the war if people ask for one. At the end, if it does not find one, it will create one. And that will not be the first time. What if the United Nations Security Council says tomorrow that it is okay to go to war? What if the inspectors find some nuclear material? Would one gram of plutonium or a ton of it be enough to start the war? What if someone comes and says that there is a link between 9/11 and Iraq? (And of course that person most likely would be speaking "on condition of anonymity"). What then, should the war start?

We need to realize that there is absolutely no justification for this war. This war not only risks global catastrophe because it involves the boiling region of the Middle East, an area perhaps more unstable than any other in the world, but it is also immoral and illegal.

It is immoral because it punished millions of innocent civilians ten years ago, has been punishing them continually since that time, and will punish them again.

It is illegal because Congress gave the illegal authority to the President of the United States to commit aggressive war. For this same kind of war, Nazi and Japanese leaders were held accountable at the Nuremberg and Tokyo trials following World War II. It is also illegal under international law because there is no evidence that Iraq plans to attack the United States.

Aggressive war is one of the most serious transgressions of international law. Nothing but organized non-violence can check the organized violence of the American government for now and in the future, if there is going to be a future.

Father Roy Bourgeois
and Howard Zinn

February 28, 2003

Here are thoughts from a letter written by combat veteran, Father Roy Bourgeois addressed to his Brothers and Sisters in the military:

> Years ago, I went to war in Vietnam to stop the spread of communism. I did not question our leaders who told us our cause was noble. The violence, death and destruction had a great impact on my life. Today, I see war as evil and a crime against humanity. As a person of faith, I believe a loving God calls each of us to be healers and peacemakers in our world. Psalm 33 says it very well:
>
> > *Rulers are not saved by their armies.*
> > *Nor can they find hope in their weapons.*
> > *Despite their power, they cannot bring peace.*
>
> I respectfully ask you to think seriously about not going to war. Refuse to kill! For those you kill will be your brothers and sisters. I plead with you as Archbishop Oscar Romero, assassinated by soldiers trained at the School of the Americas, pleaded with the military of El Salvador:
>
> > *When you hear the words of a man telling you to kill, remember the words of God: 'Thou shall not kill!' No soldier is obliged to obey an order contrary to the law of God. In the name of God, in the name of our tormented people who have suffered so much and whose laments cry out to heaven, I beseech you, I order you in the name of God, stop the repression!*
>
> I know what I am asking you has serious implications for each of us. I also know that following the ways of God can bring us peace, hope and deep inner joy. Following those who send us to war will only bring death and destruction.

To add some thoughts from Howard Zinn:

Yes, we support our troops, we want them to live, we want them to be brought home. The government is not supporting them. It is sending them to die, or to be wounded, or to be poisoned by our own depleted uranium shells.

Aside from soldiers refusing to serve, we must call upon journalists who are tired of being manipulated by the government . . . and who will begin to write the truth. The power of our rulers depends on the obedience of citizens, of soldiers, of civil servants, of journalists and writers and teachers and artists. Once these people realize that they have been deceived and withdraw their support, the government loses its legitimacy and power. This government came into power by a political coup, not by popular will.

We must ask the incompetent Mr. Bush to step down. We must continue the process of impeachment. No blood for oil, no blood for Bush, no blood for Rumsfeld or Cheney or Powell, no blood for the grandiose designs of empire.

What is being planned is not a war at all. It is primarily a massacre of children. The average age in Iraq is 14 years. The first Iraq War was a massacre which has actually never stopped as the daily bombing of the innocent continues.

Project for the
New American Century

March 7, 2003

We find ourselves at a moment of international crisis. We have suffered through a political coup and continuing criminal behavior on the part of our government. They have plotted and planned to conduct a second massacre in Iraq. Iraq One was a massacre and Iraq Two will be a bigger massacre. Neither can be correctly called a war.

They are currently misusing our hard earned tax money to bribe any and every nation they can to come on board their criminal enterprise. These are high crimes and misdemeanors.

Who are these people? The Project for the New American Century, (PNAC) is a Washington-based think tank created in 1997. Their objective is the establishment of a global American empire bringing the world together under the umbrella of a new socio-economic Pax Americana.

After Bush was selected, the people who created PNAC became the rulers of the Pentagon, the Defense Department and the White House. When the Twin Towers came down, the PNAC people saw their chance to turn their predetermined agenda into government policy.

The PNAC statement of principles is signed by Cheney, Wolfowitz, Rumsfeld, Elliot Abrams, Jeb Bush and Bush special envoy to Afghanistan Zalmay Khalizad. William Kristol, writer for the Weekly Standard, is also a cofounder of this group. The Weekly Standard is owned by Robert Murdoch, who owns Fox News. Yes, Richard Perle is also a PNAC member.

In opposition to the imperial goals of PNAC which has now morphed into the Bush Administration, there is the international movement for justice and peace. Never before has the peace movement been so visible and so effective.

If we continue to lead, our "leaders" will follow. This is what took place in the civil rights movement. Life long segregationists finally got "religion" when they realized their racist game was up. And today life long militarists must begin to realize that the slaughter they so love has created international disgust and rejection.

Reasons for George Bush to Resign:

- Lying to the people he was supposed to serve.

- Planning to invade Iraq regardless of its elimination of weapons of mass destruction.

- Reckless endangerment of the people of the United States and the people of the world.

- The implication that the coming massacre will be good for Israel.

Project for the
New American Century
II

March 14, 2003

Attorneys are bringing Tony Blair's case to the new International Criminal Court today. They believe he is involved in planning, preparing and conspiring to commit an international crime. Similar charges could be brought against George Bush but the United States is not a party to the new International Criminal Court. If Mr. Bush ever travels outside the United States, however, he could be subject to the Universal Jurisdiction of the Court.

So instead of seeking the same indictment that is sought against Tony Blair, a Bill of Impeachment will be brought to the House of Representatives. If Bill Clinton could be impeached for his sexual dalliance, it seems that someone preparing an international massacre should be impeached *a fortiori*, that is, for a greater reason. Neither Iraq One nor Iraq Two will be categorized as wars. Both will be recorded by history to be massacres. We have suffered through a political coup and continuing criminal behavior on the part of our government. Currently our hard earned tax money is being used to bribe any nation to come on board their criminal enterprise. These are high crimes and misdemeanors.

This current cabal came from the Project for the New American Century, (PNAC) a Washington-based think tank created in 1997. Its objective is the establishment of a global American empire bringing the world together under the umbrella of a new socio-economic Pax Americana. After Bush was selected the people who created PNAC became the rulers of the Defense Department and the White House. When the Twin Towers came down the PNAC people saw their chance to turn their predetermined agenda into government policy.

The PNAC statement of principles is signed by Cheney, Wolfowitz, Rumsfeld, Elliot Abrams, Jeb Bush and Bush special envoy to Afghanistan Zalmay Khalizad. William Kristol, writer for the *Weekly Standard*, is also a cofounder of this group. The *Weekly Standard* is owned by Rupert

Murdoch, who owns Fox News. Yes, Richard Perle is also a PNAC member.

In opposition to the imperial goals of PNAC there is the international movement for justice and peace. Never before has the peace movement been so visible and so united.

Rachel Corrie

March 20, 2003

Three isolated men on an isolated island decided to conduct a holocaust, a crime against humanity, a massacre. This will be known as the children's holocaust because the majority of the victims will be children.

Citizens of the United States have been betrayed by a Congress and a President, that are of the corporations, for the corporations and by the corporations. "Fascism," said Mussolini, "should be more properly called corporatism, since it is the merger of state and corporate power." And friends, the corporations are paid for the material of war and then they will be paid again for reconstruction of the fifty-first state after the war.

We want our country back. We want our hard-earned tax money to go to education, health care and the reestablishment of the public sector, which has been systematically destroyed. Taxation without representation is tyranny. We must not be paralyzed by this act of crass terror that is taking place as we speak. Each of us must engage in the resistance in accord with our ability and our conscience. Our non-violent international revolution for peace and justice has begun. We must vigil, march, protest and picket daily. Our core organization is many million strong. We must be more creative than ever before.

Rachel Corrie . . . ¡Presente, Presente, Presente!

Here is part of Rachel's letter to her parents just before she was crushed to death by an Israeli bulldozer:

> I don't know if many of the children here have ever existed without tank-shell holes in their walls and the towers of an occupying army surveying them constantly from the near horizons. I think, although I'm not entirely sure, that even the smallest of these children understand that life is not like this everywhere. An eight-year-old was shot and killed by an Israeli tank two days before I got here.

They know that children in the United States don't usually have their parents shot and they know they sometimes get to see the ocean. But once you have seen the ocean and lived in a silent place, where water is taken for granted and not stolen in the night by bulldozers, and once you have spent an evening when you haven't wondered if the walls of your home might suddenly fall inward waking you from your sleep, and once you've met people who have never lost anyone—once you have experienced the reality of a world that isn't surrounded by murderous towers, tanks, armed "settlements" and now a giant metal wall, I wonder if you can forgive the world for all the years of your childhood spent existing—just existing—in resistance to the constant stranglehold of the world's fourth largest military—backed by the world's only superpower—in it's attempt to erase you from your home. That is something I wonder about these children. I wonder what would happen if they really knew.

And a thought from the Talmud (the collection of Jewish law and tradition consisting of the Mishnah and the Gemara):

Do not be daunted by the enormity of the world's grief. Do justly, now. Love mercy, now. Walk humbly, now. You are not obligated to complete the work, but neither are you free to abandon it.

The struggle for peace and justice continues.

What follows is a portion of Rachel's letter that I did not have time to read on the air:

As an afterthought to all this rambling, I am in Rafah, a city of about 140,000 people, approximately 60 percent of whom are refugees—many of whom are twice or three times refugees. Rafah existed prior to 1948, but most of the people here are themselves or are descendants of people who were relocated here from their homes in historic Palestine—now Israel. Rafah was split in half when the Sinai returned to Egypt.

Currently, the Israeli army is building a fourteen-meter-high wall between Rafah in Palestine and the border, carving a no-man's land from the houses along the border. Six hundred and two homes have been completely bulldozed according to the Rafah Popular Refugee Committee. The number of homes that have been partially destroyed is greater.

Today, as I walked on top of the rubble where homes once stood, Egyptian soldiers called to me from the other side of the border, "Go! Go!" because a tank was coming. Followed by waving and "what's your name?" There is something disturbing about this friendly curiosity. It reminded me of how much, to some degree, we are all kids curious about other kids: Egyptian kids shouting at strange women wandering into the path of tanks. Palestinian kids shot from the tanks when they peak out from behind walls to see what's going on. International kids standing in front of tanks with banners. Israeli kids in the tanks anonymously, occasionally shouting— and also occasionally waving—many forced to be here, many just aggressive, shooting into the houses as we wander away.

In addition to the constant presence of tanks along the border and in the western region between Rafah and settlements along the coast, there are more IDF towers here than I can count—along the horizon, at the end of streets. Some just army green metal. Others these strange spiral staircases draped in some kind of netting to make the activity within anonymous. Some hidden, just beneath the horizon of buildings. A new one went up the other day in the time it took us to do laundry and to cross town twice to hang banners. Despite the fact that some of the areas nearest the border are the original Rafah with families who have lived on this land for at least a century, only the 1948 camps in the center of the city are Palestinian controlled areas under Oslo. But as far as I can tell, there are few if any places that are not within the sights of some tower or another. Certainly there is no place invulnerable to Apache helicopters or to the cameras of invisible drones we hear buzzing over the city for hours at a time.

I've been having trouble accessing news about the outside world here, but I hear an escalation of war on Iraq is inevitable. There is a great deal of concern here about the "reoccupation of Gaza." Gaza is reoccupied every day to various extents, but I think the fear is that the tanks will enter all the streets and remain here, instead of entering some of the streets and then withdrawing after some hours or days to observe and shoot from the edges of the communities. If people aren't already thinking about the consequences of this war for the people of the entire region then I hope they will start.

I also hope you'll come here. We've been wavering between five and six internationals. The neighborhoods that have asked us for some form of presence are Yibna, Tel El Sultan, Hi Salam, Brazil, Block J, Zorob, and Block O. There is also need for constant nighttime presence at a well on the outskirts of Rafah since the Israeli army destroyed the two largest wells. According to the municipal water office the wells destroyed last week provided half of Rafah's water supply. Many of the communities have requested internationals to be present at night to attempt to shield houses from further demolition. After about ten p.m. it is very difficult to move at night because the Israeli army treats anyone in the streets as resistance and shoots at them. So clearly we are too few.

I continue to believe that my home, Olympia, could gain a lot and offer a lot by deciding to make a commitment to Rafah in the form of a sister-community relationship. Some teachers and children's groups have expressed interest in e-mail exchanges, but this is only the tip of the iceberg of solidarity work that might be done. Many people want their voices to be heard, and I think we need to use some of our privilege as internationals to get those voices heard directly in the US, rather than through the filter of well-meaning internationals such as myself. I am just beginning to learn, from what I expect to be a very intense tutelage, about the ability of people to organize against all odds, and to resist against all odds.

Cuba Missile Crisis Revisited

April 7, 2003

Hospitals are overflowing with the wounded and dying. Cluster bombs are falling. A children's holocaust is taking place in Baghdad. It's not simply the children whose heads are blown off or torn to shreds by cluster bombs, many are shell shocked for life by the sheer concussion of bombs and missiles.

This crime against humanity must come before an international tribunal. We can easily identify the twenty or so suspects who designed this evil massacre. They must be indicted and tried for war crimes.

Most seriously, as they continue to lose, they are more apt to use nuclear weapons. As our listeners know, during the failed Bay of Pigs attack in 1961 our "intelligence" determined that Cuba would fall like an over-ripe fruit.

What a surprise, Cuba came to the defense of its head of state and repelled the poorly informed invaders. Following the absolute failure of this attempt to overthrow the government of Cuba, our "experts" turned to nuclear warfare as the next step. We came within one word of having a planet busting nuclear disaster as we went toe to toe with the Soviet Union in the Cuban missile crisis during the administration of John F. Kennedy. The fact that we did not have a nuclear holocaust was an accident. A Soviet nuclear sub commander rescinded the order to fire which had already been given.

The bellicosity of our current leadership makes nuclear war more of a threat now than it was during the Cuban missile crisis. Friends, our planet cannot sustain a nuclear exchange. The cabal that designed the Iraq massacre does not know what it is doing. We must stop the war now. Support our troops. Bring them home now.

Manipulating Fear

How about a little quiz on government? What is the purpose of our government? We are a nation based on self-government, which is the principle that the people are the ultimate source of governing authority and that their general welfare is the *only legitimate purpose of government.*

Therefore the government of the United States must not be the government of Iraq. The only legitimate purpose of the government of the United States is the general welfare of the people of the United States.

Can you name one thing that the current unelected government has done for the general welfare of the people of the United States? It seems to me that the only possible answer is, "No, I can't."

But how do you get the masses of the people to ignore the failure of government to do its job of providing for the general welfare of the people of the United States? That is done by allowing Carl Rove to be the master of fear manipulation to frighten the people so much that all they will ask from government is protection, not performance.

Did the present unelected government of the United States have any authorization to kill Iraqi children? No it did not.

Did the present governing clique have any authority to traumatize the children of Iraq for life and destroy their nervous system by shell shock? No it did not? Would you call this child molestation? Yes, I would.

Does the end justify the means? No it does not. How long will our troops be in Iraq? With Korea as an example they will be there at least 53 years. What about the people cheering regime change in Iraq? This is exactly what they did when Saddam Hussein came into power in the first place.

This is what the people of Cambodia did when Pol Pot took over that country. He subsequently killed a substantial percentage of the population. If the only legitimate purpose of government is the general welfare of the people of the United States then the current resident of the White House has presided over a vacuum.

Franklin Roosevelt included freedom from fear as the fourth freedom.

He insisted that we had nothing to fear but fear itself. But much of Mr. Bush's time domestically has been simply fostering and manipulating fear.

No one should profit from an illegal act. The temporary administration of Iraq is the legal task of the United Nations. As it stands now Iraq will simply be our Palestine. As such it will be nothing more than an ongoing disaster for the people of the United States.

Congratulations to the peace and justice movement for reminding our administration that we are a nation based on self government which includes the principle that the people are the ultimate source of governing authority and that their general welfare is the only legitimate purpose of government.

No war in Syria, no war in Iran and no war in North Korea. Should the current administration not understand this we suggest that the current incumbent follow the excellent example of Richard Nixon and resign.

Pyrrhic Victory

April 29, 2003

The international movement for justice and peace suffered a loss as a result of the recent assault on Iraq. Yes, we lost a battle. But we have been victorious in the international battle for public opinion. We have been identified as the Second Super-Power. Tens of millions made a powerful and indelible statement against war in Iraq and against war itself.

The Pyrrhic victory of US British forces in Iraq has created enemies that may turn and strike at any time in the days, weeks months and years ahead. But the peace and justice movement has created friends and solidarity throughout the world.

The Pyrrhic victors in Iraq are divided and contemptuous. Some are so addicted to the chronic failure of war they are plotting to attack, Syria, Iran, and North Korea. These people desperately need therapy. Their disease is called necrophilia, it is a contagious love of death. The movement for justice and peace, however, is promoting biophilia or love of life. This blessed movement does not use the toxic catalyst of fear. In fact this movement is aware that perfect love casts out fear.

Some people have tried to prove that the Bush Administration was responsible for 9/11. Well, just as the effort to find out who killed John Kennedy, this effort might take years to prove or to disprove. But what does not take years to prove is that the Bush Administration is responsible for the assault on Iraq including the death and injury of our troops including those who come home with Gulf War Syndrome. It is also responsible for the deaths of innocent Iraqi men, women and children. We have absolute proof of this. We do not need to pursue any alleged conspiracies. Our case is thoroughly documented.

We were deliberately lied to by our president who used the threat of nuclear war by Iraq as a reason for the war. Keep in mind that his rogues gallery of advisers will use this specious reasoning to promote any war.

While the whole world is looking for constructive 21st century leadership we are practicing 19th century colonialism. The world is waiting

105

for us to lead in abolishing weapons of mass destruction internationally.

Rather than giving attention to moral leadership, the administration is focusing on the distribution of cushy contracts to industrialists embedded in our government.

But wait, are we not forgetting that an evil dictator has been removed? Yes, but the proper removal of such people as Saddam is the rightful function of the very International Criminal Court which our administration opposes. 150 people demonstrated in Fallujah, Iraq this week. Our troops shot 15 dead and wounded another 75. A follow-up demonstration at this outrage was marked by more killing. Are we trying to compete with the methods of Saddam?

A word from President Theodore Roosevelt might help:

> To announce that there must be no criticism of the President, or that we are to stand by the President right or wrong, is not only unpatriotic and servile, but it is morally treasonable to the American public.

The Robust Nuclear Earth Penetrator

May 16, 2003

It is time to awaken your members of Congress from sleep. Insist that they stop the spread of the most dangerous weapons in history by blocking funding for the Robust Nuclear Earth Penetrator and also preserving the ban of mini-nukes. U.S. development of so-called usable nuclear weapons undermines U.S. demands that other countries not seek to acquire nuclear weapons.

If the U.S. will not lay down its nuclear weapons and stop developing new ones, why should anyone else—especially those that feel most threatened by the new U.S. policy of preventive war?

Since the end of the Cold War, some civilian military planners and nuclear scientists have argued for creating a new class of earth-penetrating nuclear weapons. These weapons are sometimes referred to as "bunker busters" because they would be designed to burrow into the ground to destroy underground military facilities that are protected by 100 to 300 feet of concrete or rock. The Robust Nuclear Earth Penetrator would use an existing nuclear weapon, redesigned for use against underground bunkers. It would have a yield of over 100 kilotons, at least seven times the size of the Hiroshima bomb.

Proponents of this monstrosity claim that, because the weapon penetrates the earth before detonating, it would be a "clean" nuclear weapon. In reality, this would be an extremely "dirty" and deadly weapon. If detonated in an urban setting, tens of thousands of people could receive a fatal dose of radiation within the first 24 hours. More would be killed or injured by the extreme pressures of the blast and thermal injuries arising from the heat of the explosion. Still more casualties would result from the fires and the collapse of buildings from the seismic shock that the explosion would produce.

Nuclear weapons proponents are also continuing to urge the development of a low-yield (approximately five kiloton) weapon, termed a "mini-nuke," which might be used against a buried bunker or on the battlefield. It is time to demand of your Senators and your Member of the House of

107

Representatives a firm NO to the proposed and illegal Robust Nuclear Earth Penetrator and a firm NO to the proposed illegal mini nukes.

The blowback from our ill fated occupation of Iraq has already begun in Saudi Arabia. The blowback from our proposed violation of international nuclear prohibitions could be the end of life on the planet.

The lawlessness of the current administration in the United States must not be given further approval by the Congress of the United States. Make it clear to your legislators that you expect them to respect the Nuclear Non-Proliferation Treaty. Failure to respect this treaty will simply encourage other nations to follow our lawless behavior.

This policy could be in the House and Senate by next week. Make that wake up call today. No Robust Nuclear Earth Penetrators and No mini-nukes either!

The Moro Islamic Liberation Front

May 23, 2003

General John "Black Jack" Pershing and his men massacred over 2,000 Moros in two brutal attacks. The first was at Bud Dajo in March of 1906 and the second was in the crater of the volcano Bud Basak in June of 1913. Both attacks were on the Island of Sulu in the Philippines.

There is no way to describe how deep the memory of these massacres remains in the minds of the inhabitants of Sulu. And now, almost a century later, our troops are moving back to the same island. We now have the largest concentration of US forces in the Philippines since the withdrawal of our military bases in 1992.

The Moro Islamic Liberation Front has been identified as our enemy thus reviving the mystique of killing Moros. The Southern Command of U.S. Headquarters is in Zamboanga on the Island of Mindanao where US forces are training Filipino commandos in so-called "counter terrorism."

Both Christian and Muslim citizens of the Philippines opposed the War in Iraq as they also call for an end to our military involvement in their country. The U.S. trained armed forces have razed villages, destroyed crops and killed livestock in a campaign of terror under the title of counter-terror. 90,000 people were displaced in the year 2000 during these joint military operations.

President Gloria Macapagal-Arroyo has become the Tony Blair of the Philippines and is compliant with the Bush Administration in spite of the opposition of her people. The 1987 Constitution of the Philippines clearly forbids foreign forces from engaging in combat on Philippine soil. In complete defiance of Philippine Law Washington states that US forces will participate in combat by operations to "disrupt and destroy" the Moro Islamic Liberation Front. George Bush once said that our we were not at war with Islam. Try to tell that to the residents of Mindanao and the Island of Sulu. It is incumbent on the current administration to prove that it is not at war with Islam.

Our war in Indochina began with sending advisers and trainers. We lost that war together with some 60,000 of our finest citizens and some 3,000,000 Indochinese civilians. The wealth and resources of our nation are being wasted on endless counterproductive military adventures. If there were any civil leadership in Washington we would work in conjunction with all nations of the earth for sane solutions. The current effort of a nation with less than 5% of the world's people to attempt to dominate the other 95% is destined to fail at the expense of the citizens of the United States.

It is difficult to distinguish the conflict in the Philippines from the conflict in Colombia—both have failed objectives and false premises. Our military presence in the Philippines, however, simply multiplies a legacy of hatred throughout the Islamic world. Anyone should know that there are as many differences within Islam as there are in Christianity or Judaism. To refer to Islam as an evil religion demonstrates a profound ignorance and mirrors the behavior of the KKK. The name of one's religion tells us nothing. There are saints and devils in every faith. By their fruits you shall know them.

Riverside Ploughshares

May 30, 2003

The gentle people of the earth are truly the most radical. They shall possess the land. On Sunday, May 25 at about 4:00 PM the Riverside Ploughshares group went aboard the warship USS Philippine Sea. They poured their blood on the missile hatches and hammered a message of protest on the containers that hold Tomahawk Cruise Missiles.

As they knelt on top of the hatches, Mark Colville held up pictures of Iraqi children who had been injured and maimed by U.S. weapons. Mark read their statement and Brian Buckley unfurled their banner which read, "Riverside Ploughshares: Disarm and Choose Life." Sister Susan Clarkson and Joan Gregory were together with Mark and Brian in this vanguard protest.

Here is their statement:

> We come here today to enflesh the prophecy from Isaiah, "They shall beat their swords into ploughshares and their spears into pruning hooks." With hammers we have initiated the process of disarming this battle ship, and transforming this carrier of mass destruction into a vessel for peace. The USS Philippine Sea uses Tomahawk cruise missiles, depleted uranium munitions and the Aegis radar system to enforce the US Empire's will on other nations and regions. We pour our blood on this ship to reveal the blood of the innocent already shed by the use of this weaponry. We also pour our blood to repent for our complicity in the pervasive violence of our world.
>
> We are trying to follow Jesus Christ's commandments to love our enemies and neighbors, to forgive those who do us harm and to repent. We seek to stop the injury of war on the human family and heal our communities by living nonviolently and seeking justice for all. The peace and security that comes from an empire wielding weapons of war and intimidation are false and illusory. With hammers we disarm this weapon of mass destruction and with blood we reveal its purpose.

111

In the spirit of Dorothy Day, who co-founded with Peter Maurin, the Catholic Worker in New York City seventy years ago, we try in our daily lives to practice the Works of Mercy. We feel that to follow God's will we must do more than serve the broken of our society. It is also our duty to challenge, as Christ did, that which causes poverty. Until we convert weapons that end life into tools that enhance life, poverty will continue to cripple our society. For this we pray and for this we act.

We are Susan Clarkson, Mark Colville, Joan Gregory and Brian Buckley from urban and rural Catholic Worker communities. Friends, not everyone is going to join these radically gentle people who represent the vanguard of the peace movement. But we can and must support them as they face severe charges in their acts of civil disobedience. In 2003 their protest is as important as the very patriotic act of those who gave us the Boston Tea Party.

Susan Clarkson
Mark Colville
Joan Gregory
Brian Buckley

Riverside Ploughshares Biographies
Fleet Week, May 25, 2003, New York City

Sr. Susan Clarkson:

I feel urged to act today because of the exposure I've had over the past three years to the charism of the Catholic Worker. The recent horrors of the massacres in Afghanistan and Iraq, the iniquitous sanctions imposed on Iraq since the first Gulf War, and my own Government's shameful alliance with the US, against the wishes of the majority of the British public, compels me to take this step of symbolic and practical disarmament, united with my American brothers and sisters.

Sister Susan Clarkson, (56) was born in Bradford, Yorkshire, England. She has been in her religious congregation for thirty-seven years and has been a member of the Dorothy Day Catholic Worker community in Washington DC, since May 2002. She sees her part in this ploughshares action as a coming together of many strands in her life: her religious vocation; peace activism in Britain; long time membership of the British Campaign for

Nuclear Disarmament; an M.A in Peace Studies; work with young people in the industrial North of England and with homeless people in London.

Mark Colville:

The example of Christ is clear: We cannot love neighbor or enemy without disarming ourselves. We cannot serve the poor without defending them against the violence of the state. We cannot affirm life without standing directly, nonviolently in confrontation with all that deals death. War is the worship of death. Preparation for war is the denial of God. Therefore I join the Riverside Ploughshares in an act of faith, offered to God as a plea for the lives of my children, and all children. Disarm. Choose Life. AMEN.

Mark Colville, 41, is a member of the Amistad Catholic Worker Community in New Haven, Connecticut. He and his wife, Luz, have been married for 13 years and are the parents of 6 children ranging in age from 7 months to 15 years. Mark's commitment to nonviolence and peacemaking is rooted in the Catholic faith and nourished by prayer and the daily practice of the Works of Mercy.

Brian Buckley:

Thank you to those who have showed us the will of the spirit through their obedience to truth and struggle for justice. To all who are victimized by our complicity, please forgive us.

Brian Buckley lives and works at Little Flower Catholic Worker farm in central Virginia. He was born and raised in Asia, and taught English in Africa with the Peace Corps.

Joan Gregory:

When falsehood and domination are so prevalent in our government, I must stand up for truth and nonviolence. We must disarm and choose life.

Joan Gregory, 70, lives at the Peter Maurin Catholic Worker Farm in New York. She was in religious life for 15 years, later married and now has two children. She has been a teacher and administrator in New York state schools and institutions for 25 years.

The Prison Industrial System

June 12, 2003

KKK members were allegedly volunteers. In place of the KKK today we have well paid members of the judiciary together with a prison industrial system that has done more harm to people of color than all of the years of the KKK combined.

One of every 32 persons in the United States is incarcerated, on probation or parole. 3,692 people are awaiting execution. Two million people are in U.S. prisons, which now make up 25% of the prisoners of the world but we have less than 5% of the world's people. In short we have more prisons, more people in solitary confinement, longer sentences and more executions than most other nations.

South of the Mason-Dixon line, incarceration rates are 12% higher than in the rest of the country. Poor African Americans and Latinos have suffered the most from this system of class justice. Poor trial representation leads to overcrowded death rows and excessive sentences. It is incumbent on judges to refuse to be rubber stamp functionaries for mandatory minimums and demand the right to judge the case.

The most serious part of this problem is political. Our judges and legislators know that "tough on crime" is a great slogan. Executing people gives our public a false sense of security just as bombing Iraq and Afghanistan have given us a false sense of security. Our archaic death penalty continues in a country that leads the world in homicide. Capital punishment is as much a failure as our ballistic foreign policy.

The average sentence for a first time, non-violent drug offender is longer than the average sentence for rape, child molestation, bank robbery or manslaughter Just as in the case of the arms business during the Cold War and the eternal Bush Wars, corporate profits are the driving forces for the prison industrial complex, which Eric Schlosser defines as "a set of bureaucratic, political, and economic interests that encourage increased spending on imprisonment, regardless of the actual need."

In short, the more prisoners there are, the higher the profits. Since

1983 we even have private, for profit prisons. The bill for the false security of prisons and the war system is paid by our deteriorating education and health programs. Mandatory sentences, primarily for drug related offenses, have filled prisons with people who 20 years ago would not have served any time at all. A mean spirited society is a failed society.

Critical Resistance: Beyond the Prison Industrial Complex drew more than 2,000 critics to its national conference in the Treme neighborhood of New Orleans. The goal of *Critical Resistance* is to end the prison industrial complex. Speakers urged those present to make the connection between protesting the prison industrial complex and fighting against both the U.S. War mania and the Patriot Act.

Let's not have profit making corporations do what is illegal for the KKK to do. Don't let incompetent legislators get your vote for false and deceptive profit making approaches to foreign or domestic security. The website for *Critical Resistance* is just that: www.criticalresistance.org.

Carl von Clausewitz's *On War*

June 27, 2003

I was fortunate to have an hour with Jonathan Schell this week. That interview will air soon on my program "World Focus" at 10:00 AM Sunday Mornings. Jonathan Schell has a new book, *The Unconquerable World: Power, Nonviolence, and the Will of the People*, published by Metropolitan Books, New York. In this book, Schell makes a historical analysis of war using examples from von Clausewitz.

Carl von Clausewitz was born in 1780 and died in 1831. His master work, *On War* has been called the greatest formal analysis of war ever made. If the five or six people who have taken power in the United States had read this book they might not have invaded Iraq. Here is the situation as described by Jonathan Schell as he interprets the analysis of von Clausewitz:

> The victor or his proconsul has taken up residency in the capital of the defeated nation. He issues an order. Do the defeated people obey? Do they "do his will?" Perhaps he thought he had won the victory when the enemy forces dissolved, but now it turns out, that decisions made by civilians far from the field of battle will determine whether he was truly victorious after all. For the war, "cannot be considered to have ended so long as the enemy's will has not been broken."

In view of the fact that the Bush administration is living in the 19th century, we might look at von Clausewitz analysis of Napoleon's invasion of Russia in 1812. Napoleon won every battle on his march to Moscow. The Russian forces retreated steadily, until he finally occupied the city—weren't the Russians beaten? All readers of Tolstoy's *War and Peace* know the will of Russia was intact. It was Napoleon who was on his way to ruin.

Leaving the comments of Schell on von Clausewitz we are forced to ask ourselves, "Is this not the history of the War in Korea? The War in in Vietnam? The Wars in Central America? The War in Panama? The War in Yugoslavia? The War in Afghanistan and of course, the ongoing War in Iraq?"

116

There is a component which von Clausewitz could not imagine, however, and that is the danger of unconscious and shallow humanoids plotting and planning the use of nuclear weapons.

Jonathan Schell believes that in the 21st Century we must look to the philosophy of *satyagraha* or living truth. The empires of the world have always known the truth. Their error has been the biblical sin against the Spirit which is to know the truth and to willingly act against it. Imperial War has never been anything less than rape, murder and terrorism all in the name of a lie. Indeed the world is unconquerable by war but it surely can be destroyed by war. Now is the time to practice direct action and non-cooperation.

Fear is contagious but courage is also contagious. Nonviolence and the will of the people are the formula for power against empire.

Humanitarian Intervention

July 9, 2003

There is a great deal of talk about humanitarian intervention at this time. Let's consider some of the components: First of all, humanitarian intervention does not have to be military. This is news to the militarists who attempt to run the world, but it is time that they understand other forms of humanitarian intervention.

The International Human Rights March planned for Israel and Palestine is a humanitarian intervention as are the actions of the tens of millions of peacemakers throughout the world.

Latrines and potable water are a humanitarian intervention. These cheapest of all facilities are the answer to many of the world's health problems. But is there ever a time that vulnerable populations need to be rescued? Of course there is. Such a situation is no different than the need for fire and police protection in any polity.

The objective, however, must not be victory over some presumed evil people and the method must not be to use religion as a cloak for malice. In a humanitarian intervention, where force is necessary, the interveners must be ready to risk their lives in the same way that fire and police do. Humanitarian intervention by force must never be "big power" intervention where selfish interests rule.

Apparently our decision makers have no contact with history beyond yesterday's *Wall Street Journal*. Nineteenth century colonialism was constantly done in the name of humanitarianism. It was done for the stated reasons of abolishing slavery, it was done in the name of improving public health, it was done in the name of civilizing and Christianizing the white man's burden. It was a façade in the name of power and resources, and that includes the pious words of President McKinley who prayed before moving on the supposed infidels in the Philippines. Having no reference point in history, George Bush stated, as quoted by Haaretz "God told me to strike at al-Qaida and I struck them, and He instructed me to strike at Saddam, which I did, and now I am determined to solve the problem in

118

the Middle East. If you help me, I will act, and if not, the elections will come and I will have to focus on them." Indeed, this is imitation Bible Speak. In the light of a fraudulent war in Iraq any talk of U.S. intervention on behalf of democracy lacks credibility.

What is to be done? The veto power of the Security Council of the UN destroys the effectiveness of the United Nations and its charter. Powerful nations like the United States are free to stop any authentic humanitarian action. The time has come for the General Assembly of the United Nations to assert itself by abolishing the Security Council. This done, humanitarian intervention, even if it requires force, can be accomplished by legitimate international law and not for the benefit of any single nation state.

Presidential Lies

July 16, 2003

There is much talk about a slip of the lip during the state of the Union message of George Bush. Was it something about Uranium from Niger for a reconstituted nuclear weapons program in Iraq?

Friends we cannot allow the accused to get away with this plea bargain of only one count. There are many other lies that must be dealt with. Lies that continue to lead our fine young men and women to their deaths. Lies that took and are taking the lives of many innocent Iraqis. Lies that continue to shred Iraqi children with scattered bomblets. This is our occupied territory. This is our Palestine.

We dropped bunker-buster bombs on the densely crowded homes of Mansour neighborhood in Baghdad killing 16 civilians including children thinking that we might kill Saddam Hussein. This act was a near exact duplication of a previous but similar attack made by Ariel Sharon as he dropped a massive bomb on a crowded Gaza slum killing 16 civilians including many children. We see stone throwers being shot down in the West Bank and Gaza and we see the same thing from our troops in Falujah. We demand an end to the torture of Palestinian prisoners at the interrogation center in Jerusalem . . . and we find prisoners being tortured to death by American interrogators in Bagram Prison in Afghanistan. And then there is the disgrace of our illegal prison at Guantanamo in Cuba. This kind of behavior will surely create suicide bombers.

And what are some of the additional lies and false implications foisted on us by the Bush Administration?

Here are a few:

• That Iraq was responsible for the September 11th attacks.

• That Iraq and al-Qa'ida were working together.

120

- That Iraq was trying to import aluminum tubes to develop nuclear weapons.

- That Iraq still had vast stocks of chemical and biological weapons left over from the first Gulf War.

- That Iraq retained up to 20 missiles which could carry chemical or biological warheads.

- That Saddam Hussein had the wherewithal to develop smallpox.

- That U.S. and British claims were supported by the inspectors.

- That previous weapons inspections had failed.

- That Iraq was obstructing the inspectors.

- That Iraq could deploy its weapons of mass destruction in 45 minutes.

- That the war would be an easy win.

- That the Shia Muslim population of Basra had risen against their Sunni oppressors.

- That our troops would face chemical and biological weapons

- That interrogation of Iraqi scientists would yield the location of weapons of mass destruction.

- That Iraq's oil money would go to the Iraqis.

- That Iraq's weapons of mass destruction were found.

- And how about that phony story about the rescue of Jessica Lynch?

Friends, these are high crimes and misdemeanors. No democracy is possible when public servants are liars.

UN Security Council

July 25, 2003

Liberia needs help. All of the mechanisms of international law are available to deliver that help. But once again the issue is diverted to a question of whether the United States should or should not send troops. Once again our narrow and nationalistic perspective creates an obstruction in the midst of a humanitarian crisis.

Should we, as the unique super-power, interact with the United Nations, the problem could be addressed and solved in a global manner. But our government and our media insist on limiting the debate as if it were national rather than an international crisis.

How can this kind of obstruction be eliminated? What is to be done? First, we need to acknowledge that we are consistently breaking a treaty known as the Charter of the United Nations. This treaty as all treaties becomes incarnate in the Constitution of the United States. To break this treaty is to break the Constitution of the United States. Second, as a member of the General Assembly of the United Nations, the United States must lead the charge to abolish the Security Council and its moribund veto power. Third, to foster the beginning of that UN restructuring by building a workable design; for example, proposing a structure whereby members of the General Assembly are selected by their nations according to population (possibly one member for every million inhabitants). Prior to serving on the General Assembly representatives would have to agree that they are not there to represent their country but to represent the people of the globe.

This means that the General Assembly of the UN will now be an international legislative entity, designed in a federal model to serve exclusively on matters that directly pertain to its jurisdiction. And that jurisdiction of the United Nations includes the mandate to assure international peace.

The International Criminal Court will have jurisdiction over individual international crimes. Aside from criminals in government, we currently have some of the world's ugliest retired dictators living comfortably in

Miami while religious nuns are facing 30 years in prison for symbolic acts of non-violence in opposition to nuclear war.

It is our task as citizens of the world's only military super-power to promote these changes rather than allowing our country to continue as the major obstacle to a functional system of international law. Please support the non-governmental organizations that are designing and demanding a restructured United Nations as a functional peace system. You are invited to share in this necessary venture.

International Criminal Court

August 1, 2003

While the Bush administration continues to relive the colonial history of the 19th century, the world is moving on without him and without us. The long sought and much needed International Criminal Court is now in session.

Luis Moreno-Ocampo is the first Chief Prosecutor of the International Criminal Court. Elected by the ratifying countries in April of this year, Mr. Moreno-Ocampo has tried criminal and human rights cases involving the extradition of a former Nazi officer from Argentina, political bribery, journalists' protection, and the crimes of the military junta during Argentina's "dirty war." Moreno-Ocampo has also been a visiting professor at Stanford University and Harvard University in the United States.

Kenneth Roth, Executive Director of Human Rights Watch says, "Too many atrocities have been committed by ruthless leaders who calculated that they could get away with mass murder . . . the International Criminal Court will help break that deadly logic."

The United States played a central role in the precursors to the International Criminal Court in the Nuremberg trials, the international tribunals for the former Yugoslavia, for Rwanda, and the Sierra Leone court. Yet, the U.S. government always demanded a high degree of control over the Court and resisted its authority to prosecute U.S. military and government officials. President Clinton authorized signing — but not ratifying—the Rome Statute on December 31, 2000, just before leaving office and on the deadline set by the statute.

In May 2002, a new position emerged as the Bush administration nullified the United States' signature on the Rome Statute. In so doing, the administration withdrew U.S. support for the creation of the International Criminal Court and asserted the exclusion of U.S. citizens from the Court's jurisdiction.

After unsigning the Rome Statutes, the U.S. government passed domestic legislation withholding military aid from countries that ratify the ICC unless they agree not to turn over U.S. citizens or employees to the

Court. The legislation also authorizes the U.S. President to use "all means necessary and appropriate" to free U.S. personnel detained by the ICC. In June of this year, the U.S. insisted that the UN Security Council extend immunity from ICC prosecution for its peacekeeping forces.

The Court can consider genocide, crimes against humanity, or war crimes which occurred after this date and which are not being tried in a national court. The ICC is independent of the United Nations and is funded by the ratifying states. The Court is housed at The Hague in the Netherlands.

Anniversary of Hiroshima

August 8, 2003

The Mayor of Hiroshima, Tadatoshi Akiba, says that Washington's apparent worship of "nuclear weapons as God" is threatening world peace. And that worship is taking place this week as our nuclear war people meet to plan some great new models of nuclear obliteration. Indeed war normalizes insanity. And the plan to use nuclear weapons preemptively in a war is a double insanity Anyone plotting, planning or conspiring to commit nuclear warfare should charged, convicted and imprisoned. If such mental perverts do not annihilate millions of people overseas, it is quite possible they will be responsible for a nuclear accident which will annihilate millions at home.

After months of babble about weapons of mass destruction in Iraq, we have found the actual program for the deployment of weapons of mass destruction right here in our country. Yes, they are preparing to build new nuclear weapons and resume nuclear testing. The plan calls for developing "more useable" nuclear weapons. They are threatening both nuclear and non-nuclear nations.

Friends, its time to realize that we have used nuclear weapons every year since 1945. How? We use them the same way a bank robber uses a pistol to get money from the teller, takes the money and does not pull the trigger. He used a pistol and we have used nuclear weapons in the same fashion for 58 years. By some miracle we have not pulled the trigger. But now we have decided to make these planet busters more useable. That simply means they are more likely to be used.

I have seen Hiroshima and I wish everyone could hear the bell toll at 8:15 AM on August 6th which marks the moment an atomic bomb from the United States abolished the beautiful city which is 429 miles southwest of Tokyo. For 60 seconds, tens of thousands of survivors and visitors from around the world bow in silence to commemorate the 160,000 people who were killed and injured in that crime against humanity.

Mayor Akiba referred to the "blazing hell fire that swept over this

126

very spot 58 years ago," and called all nuclear weapons, "utterly evil, inhumane and illegal under international law."

Let's get it very clear, the testing and production of nuclear weapons is a reckless endangerment of the people of the United States and the rest of the people on this small planet. There is no security in building new nuclear weapons. Our security lies in abolishing the world's nuclear arsenal, not in building new threats to our existence.

Chalmers Johnson's
The Sorrows of Empire

August 15, 2003

The United States has deteriorated tremendously under the current administration. We are a polity isolated from the rest of the world and now an object of international hatred. Chalmers Johnson foresees four sorrows to be visited on this United States. Their cumulative effect guarantees that the United States will cease to resemble the country outlined in the Constitution of 1787.

The first sorrow is a state of perpetual war, leading to more terrorism against Americans wherever they may be. There will be a spreading reliance on nuclear weapons among smaller nations as they try to ward off the imperial juggernaut. The second sorrow is a loss of democracy and Constitutional rights as the Presidency eclipses Congress and is itself transformed from a co-equal executive branch of government into a military junta. The third sorrow is the replacement of truth by propaganda, disinformation, and the glorification of war, power and the military legions. The fourth sorrow is bankruptcy, as the United States pours its economic resources into ever more grandiose military projects and shortchanges the education, health and safety of its citizens.

There is a warped religiosity in all of these actions by the Bush government. He seems to have equated himself with Jesus in his repeated comments that those who are not with us are against us, which is a duplication of Matthew, Chapter 12, verse 30. "He that is not with me is against me."

Or, as the Israeli newspaper Haaretz quotes Bush saying, "God told me to strike at al-Qaeda and I struck them, and He instructed me to strike Saddam, which I did . . . ." So much for imitation Bible Speak.

Allegedly there were some 148 of our troops killed in Operation Desert Shield and Operation Desert Storm in 1990-1991. 696,778 service people served in these operations and now an astounding 168,001 veterans have been classified as "disabled." The casualty rate for the first Gulf war is a staggering 29.3% of the total number of troops. Thanks to Chalmers Johnson for this data and we look forward to his new book on the *Sorrows of Empire*.

How do we turn these sorrows into joy? It is time to send our troops home from Iraq, our Palestine, our occupied country, and to put the temporary administration of Iraq into the hand of the United Nations with a view to granting sovereignty to the Iraqi people. The families of our troops are in favor of this. Let's support those families as we demand the immediate return of our troops. As we look to the relationship of our President to the troops and to the people of Iraq, we must say, "He lied . . . they died."

Blowback in the Middle East

September 5, 2003

The parallel between Israel and the United States is ever more clear. Millions of Israelis are being ignored just as hundreds of millions of U.S. citizens are being ignored. The policies of the Likud Party and the Republican Party have much in common. Advisers to George Bush seem to clearly represent the Likud Party. Likud is as antithetical to the people of Israel as our current administration is to the people of the United States.

Critical thinking is required. Israel and the United States are losing the best of their citizens every day. Palestine and Iraq suffer even more as victims of occupation. Both Israel and the United States have the power to end the occupations. By ending the occupations there would no longer be a daily body count of our own citizens, Israeli citizens, Palestinians and Iraqis.

Neither Iraq nor Palestine has the power of the United States and Israel. It is the duty of the powerful to end the bloodshed. The people of Israel suffer daily because of their inept leadership and similarly the members of our armed services and our citizens at home suffer unnecessarily because of criminality and corruption in our government.

Think about it . . . conventional wisdom is so convoluted that it uses the word positive for uncritical acceptance of every wrong-headed act done by our government in conjunction with Israel.

However, what is truly positive is to look at reality with a critical eye and demand change. Conventional wisdom is the useless babble designed to make our citizens into mental vegetables.

Without critical thought, no democracy is possible. A lack of critical thinking means the continuation of unnecessary wars. The double speak of war has corrupted our language. Failure to discern is the function of an unconscious mind. The developed human person is capable of critical thought and failure to think critically is a failure to be human.

Israel's behavior toward Palestine has led to a predictable blowback. U.S. behavior in Iraq has also led to a predictable blowback. No group of people is anxious to be occupied by a foreign power with zero understanding and zero respect for their culture.

The very people telling you that war is peace are also trying to tell you that negative is positive. If, however, you oppose the ignorance of imperial behavior, you are truly positive.

The commercial media and the lifeless victims of its propaganda represent a negativity in our culture. Let's develop our critical thinking ability and become positive intellectual adults.

The Definition of a "ProAmerican"

September 15, 2003

The defunct World Trade Organization was truly unAmerican. Congratulations to Starhawk and the poor of the earth who cast the mighty from their seats. By the way, what is an "unAmerican?" An "unAmerican" is someone who thinks we have a king and who believes in the divine right of kings.

Such an attitude is required for giving homage to the current resident in the White House. In short, I think an "unAmerican" would give uncritical acceptance to political authority as if it were their religious faith. Actually, I think an "unAmerican" would make the United States into an idolatrous religion.

I think an "unAmerican" would confuse this nation's policies with the Super Bowl and insist on being a cheering section for our side regardless of the facts. It seems to me that an "unAmerican" would be concerned about personal wealth and absolutely unconcerned about the common good, the public good and distributive justice.

Well then what is a "proAmerican?" I think a "proAmerican" is someone who understands that political leaders are to be a servant class for all of the people and that they must never forget their place in society. A "proAmerican" would thoughtfully question authority and especially that of any framers of mean spirited and vengeful policy directed at individuals or groups. A "proAmerican" must have some sense of history and current events. There simply cannot be a "proAmerican" who lacks a sense of the common good, the public good and distributive justice.

I think a "proAmerican" would be ever conscious that America extends from the North Pole to the South Pole in the Western Hemisphere and that one section of America is called the United States.

"ProAmerican" people must value the lives of those outside of our polity as much as they do those who live within it. It seems to me that to be "proAmerican" we must understand that the most serious danger to our future are groups like the World Trade Organization which have such a minimal understanding of democracy that they will impoverish the many in order to have a wild excess of greed for the few.

A "proAmerican" would understand that we live on a very small planet which is currently in very grave danger. In short, we live on a life boat in space. If we drill holes in the forward section of the boat, we who live in the aft section will sink together with the rest.

Once again conventional wisdom has it all backwards. Conventional wisdom is apt to call someone "proAmerican" who is in fact a racist, war mongering fanatic. There is no future for such thinking. May the World Trade Organization rest in peace. God Bless the whole world, no exceptions!

Bush's Preventative War

September 26, 2003

George Bush was talking to himself as he stood before the United Nations. He spoke about weapons which we have and use and he said this must be stopped. Yes, it must. George spoke of stopping great threats before they arise. This was a clear reference to preventative war and, as international legal scholars know, preventative war was the "supreme crime" condemned at the Nuremberg Trials of the Nazi war criminals. George then diverted our attention from his illegal war and fraud by speaking about sex slavery.

He reminded me of a guilty person telling the judge and jury that there are other serious crimes and other criminals, and saying, "Why me?" Sex slavery is a serious crime and must be addressed but that is not the charge directed at Mr. Bush at this time.

Senator Edward Kennedy said the case for going to war against Iraq was a fraud and that the Bush administration has failed to account for nearly half of the four billion dollars the war is costing each month. Kennedy said he believes much of the unaccounted for money is being used to bribe foreign leaders to send troops to Iraq.

Historian Arthur Schlessinger says that the Bush policy is, "Alarmingly similar to the policy of Imperial Japan at the time of Pearl Harbor." Schlessinger said, "The global wave of sympathy that engulfed the U.S. after 9/11 has given way to a global wave of hatred of American arrogance and militarism and the belief that Bush is a greater threat to peace than Saddam Hussein."

Regime change begins at home!

The Refuseniks

October 3, 2003

An international movement for justice and peace made its voice clear this week in Los Angeles, London, Paris, Seoul, Cairo, Warsaw, Brussels, Stockholm, Ankara, Beirut, The Island of Crete, and in Spain in Madrid, Barcelona, Seville and Malaga.

Just a few months ago, our government was calling the United Nations irrelevant; and now we are on our knees asking for help. Irrelevant indeed. Our occupations have led to ongoing guerrilla warfare in Iraq, Afghanistan and Palestine. The occupations have been a failure. The imposters in our government who have designed this terror must be held responsible. George Bush has earned the name of his predecessor, Rutherford Hayes, who was also a selected President and through the four years of his miserable presidency was known as "Your Fraudulency."

Can you smell a slight shift in the commercial media? They are starting to follow the lead of those of us in the streets. Perhaps they can see the dramatic increase in poverty and unemployment. Perhaps they can see that every day fewer people have any claim on the current shoddy health care programs designed solely for windfall profits. And such bankruptcy is the legacy of militarism.

Not only are shifts obvious in the commercial media, we continue to see dramatic shifts among the people of Israel. The speaker of the Israeli Knesset from 1999 to 2003, Avraham Burg, has published a major article called "The End of Zionism." He states that the Zionist revolution has always rested on two pillars: a just path and ethical leadership. He insists that neither of these pillars are operative any longer.

The refuseniks within the Israeli military are growing every day. Courage to Refuse is a group of officers and soldiers who refuse to serve in occupied Palestine. And now the Israeli Air Force is in a posture of refusal as well. They have described the aerial activities in the territories as illegal and immoral. Here is their statement: "We have decided to obey the order that obliges us not to carry out an order that is blatantly illegal."

135

Friends, we are winning in the war against war. Our own disillusioned, depressed and despondent troops occupying Iraq and Afghanistan are now making similar statements. Regime change begins at home. This regime has betrayed the people of the United States and has become a threat to our survival. We must recall the President. Recall the misleader.

Get used to victory friends. We are winning.

Sharon and the "Anti-Semitism Virus"

October 10, 2003

Mr. Bolton has taken up the faded script used to create the war in Iraq. He has simply erased the name Iraq and substituted the name Syria. He is fostering ignorance and malice to prepare the way for another slaughter, another disaster in the face of our failures in Afghanistan and Iraq. We now hear talk of Syria's weapons of mass destruction and all the other pre-war lies applied to Iraq. The same script, the same allegations and the same demonizations. The first acts of war on Syria have begun.

And Israel retains its freedom to bomb Syria or any other country as long as its gets the O.K. from our government. And it has received that O.K. together with a warning, "Now, now if you bomb Syria and Gaza a hundred more times we might restrict a few of your privileges and then again, we might not."

I would really like to see an end to all suicide bombing in Israel immediately. But it seems that a misguided and misleading non-leadership in our country is supporting a policy that will simply multiply attacks on Israel. If we would only listen to Israeli intelligencia as they speak so clearly on this matter. Take, for example Uri Avnery of Gush Shalom who writes, "The State of Israel is causing the resurrection of anti-Semitism all over the world, threatening Jews everywhere. The Sharon government is a giant laboratory for the growing of the anti-Semitism virus."

Sharon's propaganda agents are pouring oil on the flames, accusing all critics of his policy of being anti-Semites . . . Many good people, who feel no hatred at all toward Jews, but who detest the persecution of the Palestinians, are now called anti-Semites.

The practical upshot: not only does Israel not protect Jews from anti-Semitism, but quite the contrary, Israel manufactures and exports anti-Semitism that threatens Jews all around the world. These words are taken from the article *Manufacturing Anti-Semites* by Uri Avnery, an Israel Peace Activist (see the website www.gush-shalom.org).

Just as our government does not represent the people of our nation, it

137

seems quite obvious that the same is true in Israel. The bombing of Syria is an opening salvo on another unnecessary and counterproductive war that will further endanger the people of the United States and Israel, not to mention innocent civilians in Syria.

History has validated the amazing work of the peace movement in the United States for decades. That peace movement is now international. We welcome the brilliance of the Israeli Peace Movement. As in our case, history will validate and approve that movement and not that government.

The Reconquest of Latin America

October 16, 2003

Friends, we are witnessing a great international revolution. The reconquest of Latin America is well underway. The Aymara and Quechua of Bolivia are telling US educated President Sanchez de Lozada to resign. (And he did resign). This is not an indigenous separatist movement. This is a movement of oppressed people. The currents are obvious in Haiti, Venezuela, Argentina, Ecuador, Brazil, Colombia, Mexico, Cuba, Paraguay, Central America and the Caribbean.

But the most significant is Bolivia. Here is where princes are being pulled down from their thrones and the lowly exalted. Here is where the hungry will be filled with good things and the rich sent away empty. In predictable fashion, the Bolivian government has responded with slaughter and support from the U.S. Embassy. Is this any different than our support of Israel as it continues its oppression in Palestine? Is this any different than a policy which creates suicide bombers in Iraq?

Come with me in spirit today into the Cathedral in La Paz, Bolivia . . . La Paz . . . The Peace. Here we find the poorest people in the hemisphere. Here we find the best organized people in the hemisphere. How I wish we in the US could trade our affluence for the organizing skills of the Bolivians. Here in the La Paz Cathedral, the Latin America of the future is present.

These non-violent revolutionaries are on a hunger strike . . . a fast. Here is their statement:

> Concerned by the government's repression and violence against social sectors in protest, and in the face of a deep political crisis that has paralyzed Bolivia, we declare ourselves in hunger strike, and:
>
> 1. We demand the immediate cessation of all repressive actions of the government against the people.
>
> 2. We exhort the mobilized social sectors in protest to put aside actions that would lead to further violence, and opt for peaceful forms of

139

struggle in defense of democracy.

3. We call for the immediate resignation of President Gonzalo San-
    chez de Lozada, to allow for a constitutional succession and the
    conformation of a government of national unity, presided over by
    the Vice President of the republic.

4. We call on the Armed Forces and the Police to follow their con-
    stitutional mandate, to defend public security, human rights and
    democratic liberties which are under threat by an irrational effort
    to suffocate popular discontent.

5. We call on citizens committed to democracy to join this initiative
    and to expand the hunger strike all over the country in temples and
    parishes in every neighborhood, until will achieve justice, peace
    and unification of all Bolivians. We take this extreme measure with
    full responsibility and honesty. We are determined that the path of
    our struggle must be peaceful.

Friends, please demand that your government stop its interference in the
hopes and desires of the Bolivian people.

Apartheid in Gaza

October 24, 2003

On Tuesday, October 21, 2003, 144 nations of the General Assembly of the United Nations condemned the apartheid wall being built by Israel and demanded that it be torn down. Israel claims that this wall will deter suicide bombers. On the contrary, it will serve to create more of them.

The Israeli Peace movement is in a similar situation to the peace movement in the United States. Lies are told by their government and those lies are promulgated by way of international media. The peace movement in Israel as in the United States is not given similar attention.

The wall is from 198-330 feet wide. This includes razor wire, two-thirteen foot deep trenches, two frontage roads, the wall itself and more razor wire. At this moment, 500 bulldozers and earthmovers are carrying out the largest national project in Israel. This immense complex—walls patrol routes, trenches, electronic barriers and sensors—is erected deep within Palestinian land.

Two million dollars are being spent for every kilometer as the Sharon government tries to redraw the border permanently. This counter productive action has no more support from the Israeli people than does the Bush tax cuts for the wealthy. The apartheid wall is 370 miles long. It is surely clear that there would be no wall at all without the approval of the Bush government.

First, our government permits Israel to oppress the Palestinians, then the Palestinians respond in predictable fashion. Then as the Bush government occupies Iraq, it imitates the failed policies of Israel and receives the same predictable resistance. The tail has wagged the dog.

The wall was begun inside the West Bank in June of 2002 . . . It has been falsely declared a "security barrier," but what is the wall in fact? It is the largest land grab since the occupation in 1967. When completed it will represent the taking of 50% of the West Bank by the Israeli government. The wall is designed to annex West Bank land on which illegal Israeli settlements were built and it confiscates prime resources as it turns the

141

West Bank into a series of cantons and enclaves in a *bantustanization* of the area. The wall has already taken over the lands of dozens of Palestinian communities and stolen the livelihood of thousands of families in the northern West Bank as well as the in areas of Jerusalem and Bethlehem.

On November 9th, 1989, the Berlin Wall was torn down. In commemoration of that achievement there will be a world wide day of action by many of the 144 nations who voted to abolish the apartheid wall.

Mr. Sharon . . . tear down that wall!

Sowers of Death and Destruction

November 4, 2003

As you look at the front page of today's *New York Times*, you see a teenager throwing stones. This teenager is in Iraq. It is hard to distinguish between Iraq and Palestine by observing the picture as Israel and the United States continue practicing the same static policies.

Historians will have a very hard time giving any evidence of peaceful mass demonstrations being mistaken. Actually, in the light of history, such mass mobilizations are almost infallible. And such is true when 100,000 Israelis come out together with fighter pilots who refuse to fly, calling air strikes on Gaza "illegal and immoral." And such is true when key elements of their military refuse to serve in occupied territory.

The Israeli Army's Lieutenant General Moshe Yaalon also buoys up demonstrators by his statement that innocent Palestinians are being harmed and that Sharon's policy is creating hopelessness and anger that work to Israel's detriment.

Here are some observations of senior Israeli intellectual Uri Avnery regarding settlers in the occupied territory:

First, one or two mobile homes are set up on a hillside. The government then claims these structures to be illegal. Then the army sends troops to defend the Israeli citizens living in the outpost.

The outpost is quickly connected to water, electricity, and telephone networks.

Next, large stretches of cultivated Palestinian lands in the area are expropriated by the military governor.

A bypass road is built taking even more stretches of Palestinian land to allow for the safe movement of the settlers and soldiers. The road with its "security area" is 60 to 80 meters wide. Palestinians then try to attack the settlement that stands on their land.

To prevent attacks on the settlement, an area 400 meters wide around the settlement is declared a "security zone" closed to Palestinians. The olive groves in fields in this area are lost to their owners. This provides the motivation for more attacks.

For security reasons, the army uproots all trees that might afford cover for an attack on the settlement or the road leading to it. The army then destroys all buildings from which the settlement or the road could be attacked.

For good measure, all buildings from which the settlement can be observed are also demolished.

Anyone who comes near the settlement is shot.

This way the settlement sows death and destruction in an ever-widening circle. The life of the Palestinian villages in the neighborhood becomes hellish. They lose the sources of their livelihood. Hundreds of such villages find themselves trapped between two or more settlements, which close in on all sides, sometimes right up to their courtyards. Their lives and their property are at the mercy of the settlers.

This process has been going on for decades all over the occupied territories. It is a slow, continuous, day-to-day offensive, unseen by most Israeli eyes.

Paramilitarism in Iraq

November 12, 2003

One of the common characteristics of imperial behavior is the inability to learn. An empire cannot learn because it has no ability to dialogue. Why talk to people when you have raw power? What is there to talk about? You will do what we say or we will kill you. As a result, the performance of an empire is consistently static, repetitive, and counterproductive.

Now, Paul Bremer has been called to the White House to discuss our failed policy. He has already expressed what he has in mind. He will recommend the treachery of paramilitarism. He will say that we don't want the honor of our military to be dragged through the muck by a policy of summary execution, torture, and rape. He knows that our troops might not even comply with such orders. They have morals and the code of military justice does not permit such atrocities. Furthermore, such behavior can lead to mutiny.

So why don't we do what we did in Vietnam and Latin America? That's it! A paramilitary program. These people will be hired and actually given a certificate of recognition as paramilitaries. They will not be Americans. Now we can say that our military has nothing to do with massacres. It was the paramilitary and we just don't know who they might be.

I have personally seen paramilitarism in Guatemala. I asked the civilian-dressed killers who gave the authority to kill. They showed me their cards as *comisionado militar*. Yes, they were commissioned by the Guatemalan Military under the direction of the U.S. Military. The military, however, will deny any knowledge of these paid killers, torturers, and rapists.

And what about Colombia? The same drill. We asked the Commanding General in Uraba if he knew who these paramilitary were.

"They are delinquents," he said, "They are the enemy."

"But General, they are based five kilometers from here and they wear the same uniforms as your troops." They even have military helicopters

145

to bomb the Choco.

"Well, maybe they rented them," said the General.

Oh yes, I remember them in Nicaragua as well. They were called Contras. They stayed away from the Nicaraguan military and specialized in killing clergy, social workers, teachers, and other non-combatants.

Friends, the paramilitary in Vietnam, Guatemala, El Salvador, Honduras, Nicaragua, and Colombia are all the same. And they will be the same in Afghanistan and Iraq. This is the shadow military removed from any code of conduct who are unleashed to torture, rape, and conduct summary execution.

Paul Bremer, why don't you forget your paramilitary dream? It will do nothing but expand the conflict as it has done everywhere else in the world. Paramilitary actions simply represent a defeated and exhausted imperial policy of repetitive malice and stupidity.

The Iraqi Holocaust

November 19, 2003

What is the proper time for the United States to leave the disaster it has created in Iraq? Now is the proper time. No it is not very complex, it is quite simple. Go home, yes, right now.

But what would happen? Iraq has been governing itself for over 5,000 years. Tyrants come and go. Iraq is quite good at either letting them die a natural death or in the case of foreigners just throwing them out. They threw the Mongols out in 1258. They threw the Brits of after a 1917 invasion to "liberate Iraq."

And what is this talk about creating a constitution? Iraq has a constitution. It was put together in 1921 in the wake of the failed British attempt to take over the country. Just think of the contradictions. The tyrant Saddam accepted the Iraqi doctrine of separation of church and state. The tyrant Saddam accepted the liberation of women and he refused to allow Islamic religious leaders to dominate the politics of Iraq.

Indeed, this tyrant did not interfere with the right of Iraqis to health care and education. And across the sea in the United States tyrants beginning with George Herbert Walker Bush began one of the world's greatest massacres of civilians; a holocaust lasting between the time of Bush the Greater and Bush the Lesser has eliminated some two million people, mostly civilians. These massacres were initiated by 88,000 tons of bombs followed by a brutal blockade that targeted children as the enemy.

One of the differences between the tyrant of Iraq and our own tyrants is that our tyrants are incapable of delivering health care, indeed they are opposed to health care delivery and they have turned health care delivery into profit delivery for the greediest of corporations. Our tyrants cannot deliver a right to education; they can only deliver bombs. The Iraq I saw just prior to the Gulf War delivered health care and medicine to all citizens without charge.

Friends, we must stop denying what is taking place. Our finest young

147

men and women are forced into the role of being an enemy in a place where they are not wanted. They are tortured physically and mentally by the orders they have received. And for each of our young people who die, at least 20 Iraqis are killed.

We are living at a time of some of the greatest war crimes in history. We simply must get the thugs out of our government. The entire leadership qualifies for trial and conviction for murder, war crimes, crimes against humanity, crimes against peace.

As 2,000-pound dumb bombs fall on Iraq today, Ken Livingston, the Mayor of London, did not give Mr. Bush the keys to the city. On the contrary he denounced the unwelcome visitor saying that Bush is: "The greatest threat to life on this planet." Let's get our troops out of Iraq now.

Thanksgiving

November 26, 2003

We have much to be thankful for.

I am thankful that hard working people in their quest for a living wage are instructing the market owners that greed is a form of institutional violence. I am thankful for union solidarity in support of the strikers. I am thankful that the workers are making it clear that a single payer national medical system would benefit the market owners as well as employees in a win-win situation.

Now that legislation has passed to destroy Medicare we should look at the facts. Health Maintenance Organization use up to 33% of their funds for administration and profit. On the contrary, Social Security spends only 3% on administration. Medicare also spends about 3% for administration. And the medical program in that far away country called Canada spends less than 1% of its fund to administer health care to all Canadians.

I am thankful that a substantial number of our citizens can observe that the public sector of our society is being abolished by a rigid ideology of privatization combined with perpetual war making.

Indeed, our militarism is creating international guerrilla warfare. Our founders became guerrillas in the face of imperial oppression. And today I think our own people would become suicide bombers if some ignorant alien power came in to our midst . . . shredded our children with fragmentation bombs, destroyed our infrastructure and put in a pseudo-government established to steal our national resources as it confined our people with apartheid walls and summary execution.

We are currently spending about a trillion and a half dollars a year for health care. And remember, that the system favored by our Congress is based on the violence of excluding people with pre-existing conditions. Check it out. If you need help we are not here for you. We don't cover that and we don't cover that and we don't cover that.

HMO's simply do not exist to cure the sick. They exist to collect your money. You guessed it, a single payer national system would be cheaper

149

and would not be based on rejecting those who need help the most.

I am thankful that our people are beginning to connect the dots as they understand that the framers of perpetual war are treasonous to the common good of the sovereign people of the United States.

Actually I'm not only thankful for the growing consciousness of our people, I am hopeful as well that we can restore and expand the non-profit public sector, welcome distributive justice into our economy and acknowledge our interdependence with all the people of this small planet.

Happy Thanksgiving.

The Name of Our Religion

December 5, 2003

The name of our religion does not define our character. Within each religion there are saints and devils. Why then even talk about religion? Because it is a spiritual path for many people. Indeed, each religion attempts to elevate the mind and heart from the confines of the ordinary.

Many cultures have made God into an image and likeness of their particular mores. In view of the fact that religion is a cultural phenomenon, is there any room for exclusivity in its practice? I don't think so.

How then can we judge the authenticity of religious practice? Quite simply, the more we claim to know about God, the less reverent we are. Just observe the behavior of some TV evangelists on this point. When they claim to know everything about God they are simply expressing their ignorance.

Religions of the west have tried to explain too much and thereby frequently demonstrate a lack of reverence. Eastern religions are generally more reverent. They do not claim to comprehend the Almighty. Reverence stands in awe of the majesty of creation. And is there any essential conflict between authentic science and authentic religion? No. Creating such conflicts either indicates a weakness in science or a weakness in theology. For the believer, science is an attempt to better understand creation. Religion generally includes a sacred story . . . a sacred book. To understand these books we must understand figurative language, metaphor, parable, poetry and sometimes actual history.

Does this mean that all is relative? Not at all. Some things are absolute. But arguing about dogmas is a great way to waste time. In short, what matters is our life-style. Some obtain spirituality with no religion at all. Some obtain it who are not able to affirm the existence of God.

Unfortunately, many political figures use religion as a cloak for malice and a stupid excuse for war. The absolutes of spirituality with or without religion are the pursuit of justice, peace, joy, love, perseverance, fortitude, reverence, respect and all related gifts which lead us to a life of wisdom, a life of action and a life in direct contradiction to all deadly conventional materialism and warfare.

The name of our religion does not define our character. Our character is defined by our willingness to build a universal system of justice and peace.

Suicide Bombers

December 12, 2003

Where do suicide bombers come from? Actually I think they can come from anywhere on earth. It could be Dubuque, Iowa or Toledo, Ohio. I don't think suicide bombers are created by geography or ethnicity. I think they are created by oppression and humiliation. This is not a clash of civilizations, it is a desperate response of traumatized people.

Why are there suicide bombers in Iraq? Because people are victims of the same abuse which the Palestinians have suffered. The Israeli Defense Forces have now been called to send urban warfare specialists to Ft. Bragg in North Carolina at the same time that Israeli consultants are visiting Iraq. As a result of this, U.S. forces are now using the same failed tactics that created suicide bombers in the first place.

Areas of Iraq are being sealed off with razor wire. Buildings which house "suspected insurgents" are being bulldozed and bombed. These tactics create rage and rage creates suicide bombers. So we are not only supporting the manufacture of suicide bombers but we are importing trainers into the United States to expand a failed program and lead to the creation of even more suicide bombers.

One of our former intelligence officers said recently, "This is basically an assassination program. It is bonkers, insane. We're already being compared to Sharon in the Arab world and we've just confirmed it by bringing in the Israelis and setting up assassination teams."

One of the planners of this offensive is Lt. General William "Jerry" Boykin who is a deputy undersecretary of Defense. Remember him? He says that Satan wants to destroy our Christian Army. Yes, he states that our military is fighting the devil. He is about as correct in his judgment as the Grand Inquisitor.

As our tax money continues to flow into a factory for creating suicide bombers, intelligent and humane people are beginning a great peace march in Israel and Palestine. The marchers are assembling in Tel Aviv. They will visit the homes of bereaved Israeli families, they will observe

153

the separation wall, they will speak at length with the Israeli citizens who will march with them into Palestinian cities. They will visit refugee camps and demolished homes and they will prove definitively that dialogue and diplomacy are possible.

Saddam and the International Court

December 18, 2003

Iraq has been personified as Saddam Hussein for the past 14 years. Media pundits often spoke as if he were the only person living in Iraq. Over a million people have been killed in the name of seeking this one-time friend of the United States. Organized crime would never accept such a sloppy performance. The first Iraq Massacre of 1991 was entirely unnecessary and was condemned by international tribunals under the skilled direction of our former Attorney General Ramsey Clark.

The apple does not fall far from the tree. Bush, the lesser, now presides over an ongoing massacre in the wake of Bill Clinton's support for the continued bombing of Iraq together with death-dealing sanctions which killed thousands of children each month. And what about the trial of Saddam Hussein? International law is a reality. All but a few rogue states respect international law. If the United States adhered to international law there would have been no bloodshed in Israel and Palestine.

If we adhere to international law today, father and son Bush, Cheney, Rumsfeld, Bill Clinton and even Jimmy Carter could be called before the proper court at the Hague. Saddam, as defendant, could correctly state that he seized power in Iraq with U.S. approval in 1979 and how he was rewarded for moving his allegiance from the Soviet Union to the United States. Saddam Hussein could further explain how the United States encouraged and financed his invasion of Iran in 1980 creating one of the longest and bloodiest wars of the 20th century. Members of the Reagan regime would be correctly questioned on why Saddam's name was removed from the list of state sponsored terrorists in 1982.

The court could ask: Donald Rumsfeld about his chummy relationship with Saddam back in 1983 as the dictator sought further military assistance; or why in 1984 the U.S. Department of Commerce licensed the export of biological toxins to Iraq; or why there was no outrage when U.S. authorities knew that the Kurds were gassed in Halabja by our ally Saddam.

155

Saddam became the enemy because he would not privatize Iraq's oil. That industry was nationalized in 1972 and was used to pay for free health care and education in Iraq. Let the group of criminals who planned this war go before the court together with Saddam. They helped him to sustain his rotten dictatorship as long as it conformed to our policy. We must not let this crime be judged by a group of confirmed liars.

Let's go to the Hague bringing in eminent international jurists and let's get all of the criminals on the stand. If Milosevic can be sent to the Hague, why can't Saddam? Many people in Iraq are happy to be rid of Saddam . . . now they want to get rid of us.

Year-End Review

December 30, 2003

This is a good time for a review of the year 2003. It may sound contradictory, but this was the greatest year for the peace movement in the history of the world. Yes, even with the wars in Iraq and Afghanistan. Why? This year's opposition was to war itself.

We were overwhelmed in January of 2003 by the presence of 500,000 demonstrators in Washington, D.C. which was the greatest statement for peace prior to war in the history of the United States.

Following this massive witness, day to day organizing continued leading up to an international outpouring of tens of millions of people on February 15th of this year. Consistent with U.S. history, many of the most radical peace people are from the religious community. A vanguard of heroic religious people symbolically attacked nuclear weapons sites and received long and harsh sentences. Father Roy Bourgeois' huge gathering to close the School of the Americas included many who crossed the line risking prison sentences of six months and more.

Demonstrators, together with invited, delegates revealed the failure of the World Trade Organization at Cancun in Mexico. Miami was the site of a bold denunciation of the Free Trade Area of the Americas. Perhaps some don't understand that Cancun and Miami represent demonstrations for world peace. The current forced trade system is simply another facet of the war system.

And now over twelve hundred members of the Israeli military have refused to serve in Palestine as a result of their outrage at the endless oppression and humiliation of the Palestinian people.

Ironically, as such significant numbers of the Israeli military intelligently refuse to serve, as four former leaders of the Israeli Secret Police denounce the methodology of Sharon, U.S. policy dinosaurs are diligently imitating that same failed methodology in Iraq.

As a result of this, our forces are receiving exactly the same response from the Iraqi people as the Israelis receive from the Palestinians. Shia,

157

Sunni, Kurds and Assyrian Christians are united as never before in the face of brutal oppression.

This was the best year in history for the peace movement. In addition to that, the United States has demonstrated the absolute limits of a super power. Multibillion-dollar Star Wars programs do not stop suicide bombers with box cutters. Only social justice can do that.

May 2004 be our year for abolishing the war system.

Victims of War

January 12, 2004

What a wonderful achievement. There are no caskets coming into Dover Air Force Base, the military's largest mortuary. At least that is the impression one would get from our meticulously managed news media. Yes, we get a list of the dead but their arrival home is declared not to be news.

And just imagine, there are no wounded at all. This group is neither listed nor counted, nor mentioned by the media. The fantasy remains: no wounded. Adding to the wonders of war, there are no enemy casualties either. This miracle is achieved by proclamation. We simply don't count enemy casualties. That's an order. They have been declared not to exist. Witnesses in Iraq, however, state that for each U.S. casualty there are from 25-40 Iraqi casualties.

Now comes the test. Is this massive denial of dead and wounded positive or negative? A cheering section for unnecessary war would call this policy positive. Why bother with such depressing material? We want to hear more about Michael Jackson. Any person whose mind has not been shrunk by propaganda must surely recognize these omissions as disgracefully negative, treacherous, deceitful, and disrespectful of our troops and of the Iraqi people. No matter how much it hurts, no matter how painful or revolting, truth is always positive. Our militarist culture is currently trying to tell us that a Disneyland life of deception and make believe is positive and the pursuit of truth is negative.

Friends, what we must now confront is not only the fact of the returning dead service people and the destruction of their families; and not only the thousands of wounded who are currently suffering as they are brutally ignored. There is something even more insidious here. Everyone who has served in Afghanistan and Iraq is a victim for life.

They may not have visible wounds, they may not be declared mentally ill but they are victims. They and their families are victims of unnecessary war. They are victims of a corrupt and lying administration, they are

159

victims of a weak-kneed Congress and a sycophant media. Some veterans will respond with bitterness, some with alcoholism and drugs and some with spousal abuse. But all have been injured, all have had their lives disrupted. All have been morally and mentally violated.

These are the same troops that were ordered to receive toxic inoculations or face court marshal in order to create excess profits for pharmaceutical companies. Yes, they were ordered to kill to for the glory of Halliburton and Bechtel. It seems to me that the only remedy for these hundreds of thousands of victims is to spend the rest of their lives making sure that no other generation is so violated.

The No Child Left Behind Act
II

January 21, 2004

George Bush spoke about our troops deployed across the world. Friends, we are talking about well over 725 bases not counting our presence in Iraq and Afghanistan. The President said these bases are making us more secure. On the contrary, I think our militarism has made us less secure.

The CIA warned George Bush that any attacks in Afghanistan or Iraq would lead to greater danger here at home. Our policy of perpetual war does not limit terrorism, on the contrary it is terrorism of the state. A policy of "shock and awe" creates terrorists. Our victims are literally shocked into responding with furor.

George said that tax relief is working. Is that why we have lost three million jobs in the United States during his tenure in office? His tax relief is working alright. It is bankrupting the United States.

And George is still huckstering private health insurance. One and a half trillion dollars go into health care every year and much of that is nothing but sheer windfall profit for the private sector as almost 44 million people are left out of the system. But for less than is being spent now, public sector single payer health care can cover everyone including the excluded 44 million people.

George says that we are raising standards for our public schools. Throughout the country, teachers are teaching students to prepare for standardized tests that are directed at the least important areas of schooling. Gone is the quest for what is really important in schooling including; critical thinking, imagination, creativity and intuition. These are the qualities Einstein considered important.

Training students for test preparation is an anti-intellectual pursuit. Gone is the love of literature, the love of reading, the excitement of public speaking, drama, the arts and music. Just prepare the students to fill in the blanks in a rote fashion. This is not education this is training. Training can tell us how to operate a machine gun. Education tells us not to use it.

George spoke of 12 years of diplomacy in Iraq. So this is his idea of diplomacy, 12 years of bombing, twelve years of the most brutal sanctions ever imposed on any people and over a million dead. Repeat after me . . . this is diplomacy. George spoke about keeping the most dangerous weapons away from the most dangerous nations. Well, the people of the world consider us to be the most dangerous nation at this time. Adding insult to injury, George continues to build his false case for Saddam's non-existent weapons of mass destruction.

George is going to increase the funding for the National Endowment for Democracy. Please study the history of this entity which has manipulated demonstration elections around the world. And no child will be left unrecruited by the conditions of the No Child Left Behind Act which intrudes into the lives of students and considers them as cannon fodder for future futile adventures.

Perhaps the most painful thing was to observe the clappers during this performance. Just what were they clapping about? Voltaire said it well, "Those who can make you believe absurdities can make you commit atrocities."

The Church's Alienation of the Left

January 29, 2004

The Church going community is often unnecessarily alienated by secular liberals. And this one fact may lead to a Republican victory in November. Some liberals become religio-phobic. They presume that all religious people are fundamentalist and reactionary. They have forgotten or simply do not know that some of the most radical voices in US history have been religious.

Need I refer to the abolitionists, the civil rights movement, the farm labor movement and much of the contemporary peace movement. The profoundly effective work of groups based in religious conviction include The School of the Americas Watch and Ploughshares. They have taken more risks and received more convictions for their non-violent civil disobedience than any existing secular groups.

Take the case of abortion. Republicans have won many church people by their opposition to abortion. Instead of respecting the anti-abortion religious community, some liberals go on the offensive as a cheering section for abortion. Would it not be more discerning and respectful to say, "We know that abortion is an obnoxious procedure . . . an attack on what could become a fully developed person. We know that it can also be a psychological and moral trauma for the woman concerned. However, we believe that making such a procedure illegal will do more harm than good. We believe that human beings have free will and that we have a right to use conscience in our choice."

The same thinking should apply to sexual abstinence. Some liberals approach to this is, "Ha, ha, ha abstinence." Would it not be better to say, "Some young people might choose to abstain from sex until marriage. This is a sure way to avoid STD's, but perhaps the majority will not abstain, so everyone should know about ways to avoid STD's.

Is this not more respectful than the approach of, ha, ha, ha, abstinence? And what about prayer? Certainly we never want any state sponsored prayer in any school and that is why I would oppose the Pledge of Allegiance which I consider to be a prayer of the state. Any child, however, can pray in any

163

school at any time. I'm talking about personal prayer, not group prayer.

Some liberals are turning off millions of people who may vote for conservatives who are apparently more respectful of the religious community. This failing alone could be responsible for George Bush winning in November.

Cheap Shots

February 5, 2004

Opponents to Israel's occupation of Palestine are sometimes called Anti-Semites. But the vast majority of such opposition is not related to ethnicity or religion; it is related to behavior. If the actions of the Israeli Defense Forces were carried out by young Christians from Dubuque Iowa, the same opposition would be in order.

Think of how many U.S. citizens were called Anti-American during their rightful opposition to our failed policies in Korea, Vietnam, Central America, Panama, Yugoslavia, Afghanistan and Iraq.

I would hope that not one more Israeli ever be a victim of suicide bombing. I would hope that not one more Iraqi civilian or member of the U.S. military ever be a victim of suicide bombing. For the protection of citizens of Israel and Palestine and for the protection of our troops and Iraqi citizens, I think the following formula is necessary:

- It is not O.K. to destroy someone's home if their child throws stones.

- It is not O.K. to torture captives.

- It is not O.K. to send out assassination teams.

- It is not O.K. to attack and capture the families of suspected subversives.

- It is not O.K. to build apartheid walls.

- It is not O.K. to bomb buildings that might possibly house a suspect.

- It is not O.K. to permit settlers to illegally occupy substantial

165

areas of Palestine.

- It is not O.K. to cut off water and electricity from civilians as a form of collective punishment.

- It is not O.K. to endlessly humiliate people because of their ethnicity.

There is a long history of failed theocracies. Many such polities have been Christian, some have been Islamic. Personally I see no future for such states.

Madison and Jefferson knew that if our constitution declared the United States to be Christian, our nation would have and endlessly conflictive future. This is not a matter of religion or ethnicity, it is a matter of political science. States with second class citizens cannot stand. The horrors of our Civil War bear testimony to this fact and we will not be whole until we can eliminate the second class citizenship of poverty in the United States.

So, let's understand that it is a cheap shot to call the hundreds of millions of people who are opposed to the occupation of Palestine Anti-Semites. It is also a cheap shot to call the hundred of millions of people who are opposed to the occupation of Iraq "Anti-American." I recommend an article in this week's *Nation*: *The Myth of the New Anti-Semitism*, by Brian Klug.

Haiti

II

February 17, 2004

Jean Bertrand Aristide was elected in 1990. He was ousted in Haiti's thirty-second military coup seven months later. Aristide was returned to power in 1994. At that time he committed a serious sin against U.S. policy, he abolished the Haitian Army which was established during the U.S. Marine occupation from 1914 to 1934. As is the case of most Latin American armies, the Haitian military was established as a mechanism to control the Haitian people.

In 1995 US forces in Haiti refused the United Nations mandate to disarm the former soldiers. As a result of this violation of international law, some 7,000 Haitian Army officers, many trained at the School of the Americas, kept their weapons and are now trying to get their jobs back by creating the 33rd coup d'tat in Haitian History.

The Washington "Consensus of Power" in the World Bank and the IMF imposed a strangling embargo on Haiti after Aristide's return to power. In spite of the fact that Haiti is the poorest country in Latin America, more schools were built in Haiti between 1994 and 2000 than between 1804 and 1994.

Jean Tatoune, a former paramilitary leader was at the heart of the Gonaives attempt to overthrow Aristide. These armed gangs are led by the very disbanded military officers who overthrew President Aristide in his first term as they created a blood bath of terror.

Andre Apaid is a leader of the opposition coalition known as the "Group of 184." This coalition includes the leadership of the death squad FRAPH including the infamous Louis Jodel Chamblain who oversaw the death of thousands of Haitians after the overthrow of Aristide in the '90s.

The Caribbean Community known as CARICOM is willing and anxious to assist in the resolution of Haiti's current conflict. President Jean Bertrand Aristide is promoting the electoral process in Haiti. The ghosts Haiti's former army know they can only succeed by a coup. They simply do not have the popular support to win an election.

Lets us not be fooled again. The same oligarchic media and corrupt political power that gave you the rape of Iraq is trying to overthrow the legitimately elected government of Haiti. President Aristide and his democratically elected government need our solidarity now.

Bush's Policy of Terrorism and the Exile of Aristide

February 25, 2004

Mr. Bush, you are either with us or with the terrorists. A well-known and well-documented group of terrorists are attempting to overthrow the first democratically elected Haitian government. Our government knows exactly who they are and has aided many of them for years.

Haiti has enjoyed an unprecedented nine years of democracy, but the very thugs that overthrew Jean Bertrand Aristide after his landslide election in 1990 are back. These are the leaders of the 1991-1994 dictatorship which killed 5,000 Haitians and left hundreds of thousands of wounded, tortured Haitians.

Guy Philippe was in the Haitian Military during Aristide's exile. He received specialized U.S. training in Ecuador and, at U.S. insistence, was then integrated into the leadership of the Haitian Police.

Both Philippe and Louis Jodel Chamblain have received on-going U.S. assistance and have been protected by the army of the Dominican Republic despite several requests for their return to face charges in Haiti. The Dominican army also receives extensive U.S. assistance, including U.S. advisers near the Haitian border, and a year ago, a shipment of 20,000 M-16 rifles were shipped to the Dominican Republic for transfer to Haiti. Chamblain was the number two leader of FRAPH, a violent paramilitary organization founded with U.S. encouragement in 1993.

The UN, the U.S. State Department and human rights groups attribute hundreds of murders and tens of thousands of other crimes against humanity in 1993 and 1994 to FRAPH. U.S. government sources have confirmed the claims of FRAPH's top leader, Emmanuel Constant, that U.S. intelligence officials encouraged him in his activities, and paid him a monthly salary. Constant has been allowed to live freely in New York, despite a 1995 deportation order and a murder conviction in the year 2000.

Upon his return to power, Aristide abolished the Haitian Army. As he developed a police force, the U.S. refused to sell him police equipment as part of a brutal economic embargo.

169

That's right, an embargo on the poorest country in the hemisphere. Adding insult to injury in 1993, U.S. intelligence agencies helped to prepare and circulate a fraudulent report stating that President Aristide was mentally ill.

The same forces that overthrew Aristide in 1991 are trying to do it again. President Jean Bertrand Aristide is asking for international police assistance to maintain his legitimate regime. Here is a free translation of his message at a press conference yesterday. "Mr. Bush, you are either with us or with the terrorists."

Haiti: The Violent Cycle Continues

March 5, 2004

To repeat the past is to disrespect the past. The past is a maze of violence, ignorance, superstition mixed in with some really good stuff. The only way to respect the past is to refuse to repeat it.

Our children are going to repeat the past because they do not study it. How many students in high school or college would have any understanding of over one hundred military interventions by our country in as many years?

The President of Haiti is in Central Africa with his wife. He is a prisoner neither free to speak nor to travel. He has been demonized by professional liars in our government and a sycophant press. Any student of history would know that what happened this week in Haiti is actually routine.

Often, the first step is to decide that our selected victim is insane. Assistant Secretary of State for Latin America, Roger Noriega, developed this standard lie and applied it to Aristide in Haiti.

In 1953, John Foster Dulles said, "So this is how we get rid of that madman Mossadegh," after the elected Prime Minister of Iran nationalized the oil. This was the same formula used for the removal of the democratically elected President Jacobo Arbenz in Guatemala in 1954. Arbenz was flown out of Guatemala just as unwillingly as Jean Bertrand Aristide was flown out of Haiti.

As Arbenz was deposed, Castillo Armas, a public relations man for the United Fruit Company was flown in together with the Ambassador of the United States. We replaced a democratic government in Guatemala established a dictatorship, and developed one of the most brutal armies in the world under U.S. direction.

The first democratically elected President in the Dominican Republic since 1924 was Juan Bosch. He was eliminated in 1965. Lyndon Johnson sent in 20,000 troops to make sure that duly elected Bosch not maintain power.

This was the case when the great Salvador Allende, a medical doctor

171

and excellent statesman was murdered in Chile on Sept. 11, 1973. It was of no concern to Henry Kissinger that we turned Chile over a Nazi Dictator.

The same methodologies mentioned above were used to conduct a coup in Venezuela in 2002. In that case, with the support of the Venezuelan Army, the coup was reversed.

Anyone in touch with authentic history will have no doubt that Jean Bertrand Aristide is just one more victim of our country's dictatorial foreign policy. Jean Bertrand Aristide is the legitimate president of Haiti. To be ignorant of history is to be condemned to repeat it.

Aristide's Appeal for Peace

March 12, 2004

My comments this week are directly from the President of Haiti, Jean Bertrand Aristide. He spoke in Creole by cell phone to the Haitian Community of the United States from the Central African Republic. Here is a translation:

In overthrowing me, they have uprooted the trunk of liberty. It will grow back because its roots are many and deep. During the night of the 28th of February, 2004, American military personnel who were already all over Port au Prince descended on my house in Tabarre.

They told me that the foreigners and Haitian terrorists alike, loaded with heavy weapons, were already in a position to open fire on Port au Prince. And right then, the Americans stated that they would kill thousands of people and it would be a bloodbath. They said that the attack was ready to start and when the first bullet was fired nothing would stop them until they take over. Their mission was to take me dead or alive.

I told the American agents that my preoccupation was to save the lives of those thousands of people. As far as my own life is concerned, whether I am alive or whether I am dead, is not important. I was trying to use diplomacy but pressure was being intensified for the Americans to start the attack. In spite of that, I took the risk of slowing down the death machine to verify the degree of bluff or the degree of intimidation.

It was not a bluff. The National Palace was surrounded by white men armed to the teeth. My residence was surrounded by foreigners armed to the teeth. The airport of Port au Prince was already under the control of these people. The truth was clear. There was going to be a bloodbath because we were already under an illegal foreign occupation which was ready to open fire and then kidnap me. I was forced to sign a letter of resignation as I was kidnapped. When my wife and I were airborne in a military plane we did not know where we were going. When we landed we did not know where we were.

I ask every one who loves life to come together to protect each other. I

173

know that Haitians who live abroad understand what tragedy lies hidden under the cover of this coup d'etat, under the cover of this kidnapping. I know and they know if we stand in solidarity we will stop the spread of death and we will help life flourish.

Courage, courage, courage! From where I am with the First Lady, we have not forgotten what Toussaint L'Ouverture has said, that the roots of the tree of peace are alive. They can cut the tree, as they have done with the machete of the coup d'etat, but they cannot cut the roots of peace.

Friends, demand of candidate Kerry that he denounce the continuous terrorism of the Bush Administration and join Congresspeople Barbara Lee and John Conyers in calling for an independent, bipartisan commission on Haiti.

September 11th Hearings

March 26, 2004

Congratulations to the world's people as millions came out this week, not simply to oppose the war in Iraq, but to oppose war. Also this week, on Capitol Hill, high level officials from the Clinton and Bush Administrations testified before the September 11th Commission, established to investigate why the U.S. failed to prevent the attacks in New York, Washington and Pennsylvania.

Unfortunately, Ms. Rice would not testify. She was busy threatening Jamaica for welcoming President Jean Bertrand Aristide and telling that sovereign state to get rid of him, or else!

At the 9/11 hearings, we heard a craving that more unilateral military force should have been used against al Qaeda. We did not hear any opposition to preventative war. Preventative war is illegal and is the stated reason for the condemnation of the Third Reich at Nuremberg.

There was no discussion during the hearing in Washington about how we had the sympathy and support of the entire globe immediately after 9/11, and how after a few weeks of out of control violence against a nation that had no part in the 9/11 attacks, we lost the world's sympathy and became the most hated polity on the planet.

Any individual of common sense would know that our job after 9/11 was to reach out to 190 nations and say, "A terrible crime has been committed against us, please help us to apprehend the criminals responsible." We would then have had the assistance of the international community. On the contrary, we were making fools of ourselves accusing everyone who differed with Mr. Bush of being a terrorist.

And now we have Mr. Bush as a stand up comic attempting to make jokes about the missing weapons of mass destruction. At the very moment our troops are being killed in Iraq, an incompetent buffoon is joking about his incompetence. The families of our troops are rightfully outraged as their children die because of his lies.

Instead of showing any leadership, we have followed the example of our surrogate, Israel. We have made Iraq into Palestine. Members of our Congress like Lincoln Diaz Balart are proposing the assassination of Fidel Castro thereby following the example of Israel in its assassination of Sheikh Ahmed Yassin.

The net effect of Mr. Bush's tenure in office has been to make an international power out of al Qaeda. I am sure that al Qaeda will do everything possible to work for his first electoral victory.

Ridi pagliacco! Laugh clown, laugh!

Falluja

April 8, 2004

The best way to ignite the Islamic World is to bomb an important mosque. Our military has just taken that step and we have opened the gates of hell. Tensions between Sunni and Shi'a have quickly lessened as they join together against the occupation of their country.

When our forces were driven from Shuala, it was the action of Sunni and Shi'a fighting together. Pathetic comments from Press Secretary Scott McClellan blame the resistance on a small number of extremists.

Contrary to media opinion, Falluja was not a hotbed of resistance during the outset of the war. It became so on April 28th when our troops opened fire on a group of 200 peaceful demonstrators and killed 15 of them. Our military claimed they were returning, fire but a Human Rights Watch investigation determined that the protesters were unarmed. And now we have bombed the mosque in Falluja killing at least 40 people.

Not satisfied with creating a massive resistance from the Sunni, our leadership has chosen to pick a fight with the Shi'a followers of Moqtada al-Sadr. This was triggered by the closing of Sadr's newspaper al-Hawza. The paper was not closed for advocating violence.

It was closed because of an eyewitness claim that a supposed car bombing killing numerous volunteers for the New Iraqi defense forces was actually done by a US plane. It seems that if our forces were directed by Saddam himself, they could not have created such militant opposition. A loss of control is seen in Basra, Najaf, Kerbala, Nasiriyah, Kufa, Kut, Diwaniyah, Thawra, Shuala and Kadhimiyah.

And if we look to Baghdad, the people in the Shi'a slums who are now furiously resisting the Americans, still hate Saddam with a passion. They suffered under his repression, they suffered under the sanctions and they were expecting some change after the 2003 invasion.

And now Mr. Rumsfeld says we are facing a test of will. We should remind Mr. Rumsfeld that a strong will to continue a failed policy is a sign of mental collapse. Friends, we must resist this counter-productive

177

policy. From Friday, April 9th through Monday April 12th, there will be nationally coordinated emergency demonstrations in cities and towns throughout the country.

Another world is possible. Let us love one another.

For a free copy of this commentary [or any other] commentary, call the Office of the Americas at 323/852-9808 or visit the OOA web site at http://www.officeoftheamericas.org.

This is Blase Bonpane.

World Focus

Interviews

January 12, 2003 to January 11, 2004

Chalmers Johnson

I

January 12, 2003

BONPANE: Hello and welcome to "World Focus." I'm Blase Bonpane. Today we're very privileged to have with us Dr. Chalmers Johnson. Dr. Johnson is a specialist on the politics and economics of East Asia and a veteran of the Korean War. Professor Johnson served on the faculties of the University of California at Berkeley, as well as the University of California at San Diego. He has written many books on Asian subjects. One of his recent books is *Blowback: The Costs and Consequences of American Empire*. Welcome Dr. Chalmers Johnson.

JOHNSON: Thank you, it's a great pleasure to be here.

BONPANE: What a great day to have you. We've just been informed that North Korea has withdrawn from the Nuclear Nonproliferation Treaty and this announcement came from, out of all places, Santa Fe, New Mexico and Governor Bill Richardson, the former ambassador of the United States to the United Nations. Would you have a comment on this most unusual development?

JOHNSON: Well, I think that their withdrawal from the Nuclear Nonproliferation Treaty is not out of character with what they've been doing. I'd also have to say that the United States itself has so thoroughly weakened international law and the attempt to create a transnational norm to deal with global problems—everything from the Test Ban Treaty to the Kyoto Protocol on Global Warming, and the International Court of Criminal Justice that our government has denounced so vigorously—that it is inconsistent for us to sit around and ask why some other country is not obeying international norms when we have been so contemptuous of them. But I don't think that this is any more significant than the decision by North Korea over the past couple of years to respond to the Bush administration's verbally extremely belligerent policy. That is to say, we have identified North Korea as a member of the so-called "axis of evil." Last September, the United States government issued a new national security policy doctrine reserving to itself the right to launch a preventive war, and even spoke of its willingness to use nuclear weapons in pursuit of this policy. In addition, North Korea faces American troops ten miles away in South Korea, which have been there for the last 50 years. The U.S. Seventh Fleet, which is based in Japan and is nuclear capable, patrols North Korean waters and the country is daily photographed by satellite and reconnaissance aircraft. Also, given our determination to go to war with Iraq, I find it very hard to imagine why anyone sitting in North Korea would not come to the conclusion that "These people intend to attack and destroy us."

BONPANE: You know, Dr. Johnson, the North Korean statement was apparently in response to the United Nations' International Atomic Agency's resolution, which called on North Korea to readmit nuclear arms inspectors and then North Korea reiterated an earlier assertion that it has "no intention to produce nuclear weapons," and it says nuclear activities will be confined to peaceful purposes such as the production of electricity. How do you feel about that?

JOHNSON: That was the original crisis. It goes back to the fact that North Korea is a failed communist country. It was simply ruined by the end of the Cold War and by the loss of support from both China and Russia, which throughout the Cold War had competed for "favors" in North Korea. North Korea has no sources of fuel. It has to import it all, and one of the things it decided to do was begin to develop electric power through nuclear power generation. It built its reactor in Pyongyang as a power-producing reactor on a Russian model, but a serious unintended side effect was the production of plutonium, which is easily used for nuclear weapons. This created the crisis of 1994, when the Americans threatened war against North Korea, but we entered into an agreement with them then that we would build for them two separate power reactors of a design that does not produce weapons-grade material as a byproduct.

BONPANE: They had the graphite ones from the Soviet Union and they were going to put in the non-plutonium ones.

JOHNSON: Yes, exactly. And in the meantime, until these new reactors were built and functioning, we agreed to supply North Korea with fuel oil for generating electricity. In return, North Korea understood that we were also going to recognize them and engage in economic activity—that is, trade with them.

182

BONPANE: Something unusual about this is that North Korea says its seeking "a peaceful settlement through negotiations" and that they would be willing to set up a separate verification procedure with the United States, thus circumventing the U.N. inspection agency. In other words, the North Koreans want to make this a bilateral issue with the United States.

JOHNSON: Well, I think they do believe their problem is with the United States. They made an agreement with us in 1994, and we now repeatedly say they violated it. Their view is that we violated it, starting in the late 1990s, during the Clinton administration, when the American government took the position that Korea simply economically was nonviable and was going to fall apart. So we did nothing to help them.

BONPANE: Now, no other nation has withdrawn from this treaty, but North Korea wants to be a nuclear power such as India, Pakistan, Israel, all of which have nuclear weapons, but none of which are signatories to the treaty.

JOHNSON: No, they're not. But the logic of North Korea—at least what South Korea believes is their logic—is that this is still essentially a defensive reaction. The Americans like to say that deterrence no longer works, but looking at North Korea one would have to say today that deterrence not only works, it is the United States that is being deterred. The North Koreans have insulated themselves from war with the United States by having—possessing—weapons that, if they used them, would produce a holocaust in South Korea and very possibly in Japan and also Okinawa. That has caused the United States to alter its tone remarkably. I think the point of North Korea's withdrawing from the Nuclear Nonproliferation Treaty and their repudiation of the International Atomic Energy Agency is simply to say they no longer have any faith in these international agencies, particularly given the fact that the United States displays so little faith in them.

BONPANE: North Korea joined the treaty in 1985, but under pressure from the Soviet Union.

JOHNSON: When the Soviet Union built that reactor, it demanded that North Korea accept the Nuclear Nonproliferation Treaty.

BONPANE: Yes, and then we had Jimmy Carter going to North Korea to broker a deal on behalf of the Clinton administration—

JOHNSON: Well, actually somewhat over the opposition of the Clinton administration.

BONPANE: Indeed, Clinton was furious, but he apparently permitted it, or tolerated it. So the North Koreans froze their nuclear program as a result of Carter's visit in return for energy assistance from the U.S. I wonder whether Bill Richardson may be able to serve in the same capacity, although of course, he has a more difficult partisan relationship with Washington.

JOHNSON: Well, I think Bill Richardson is a somewhat bizarre choice, even though he was at one time ambassador to the United Nations. But North Korea remains a remarkably isolated place. It has so little contact with so few Americans that it probably has a list of them, perhaps on the back of an envelope, and then picks out one that it recognizes.

BONPANE: North Korea has had no diplomatic relations with the U.S. since the 1950-1953 war, which ended in an armistice and no peace treaty.

JOHNSON: North Korea has never had relations with the United States. There is a North Korean ambassador to the United Nations, and we keep contact with him. I would have to say that despite all of the American talk about this being a Stalinist regime, North Korea has a remarkable record of rationality. For example, in 1979, the South Korean Central Intelligence Agency assassinated President Park Chung Hee, and one would have thought if ever there was an opportunity for North Korea to intervene and take advantage of the great instability in the south this was it. But they did nothing. There is no doubt that North Korea does have a history of terrorist attacks against the South: killing the South Korean cabinet on a visit to Rangoon in 1980, bombing a KAL airplane, and abducting both South Koreans and Japanese in Japan. These are very serious incidents, but I'd have to say each one of them could be matched by our own CIA almost any day.

BONPANE: It's amazing that China wants a diplomatic solution and is begging the United States to have a dialogue and negotiations with North Korea. You also argue in your book *Blowback* that the U.S. is ignoring South Korea's peace initiatives toward the North.

JOHNSON: Let me say a word about the growing anti-Americanism in South Korea. When the Bush administration took over in January of 2001, the Korean situation was well on its way toward a favorable resolution. The American Secretary of State under Clinton had already been to Pyongyang. South Korean President Kim Dae-jung, because of his courageous act in going to Pyongyang and offering reconciliation, had won the Nobel Peace Prize. Had there been a few more weeks in the Clinton administration, it looked as if President Clinton was going to visit North Korea. Instead, President Kim of South Korea visited Washington in the Spring of 2001 and was badly brushed off by President Bush. He was treated rudely and insultingly and it reverberated badly in South Korea. Then the "axis of evil" speech sounded to many South Koreans as racist in that the people of North and South Korea are nonetheless all Koreans. To suggest that those north of the 38th parallel are in some way evil, sounded rather strange to people in the South.

I would also like to stress a recent incident in which two young girls who were walking along a country road just north of Seoul were crushed to death by an American armored vehicle. This was widely reported in the Korean press and not at all reported here in the U.S., and it's one of the things that has outraged the South Koreans. The two people operating this vehicle were charged with negligent homicide and tried by the American military. They offered as a defense that the internal communications mechanism between the lookout and the driver didn't work. It turned that if they had plugged in the earphone into the right outlet it worked fine. Their commanding officer was never called to testify. It was not even clear that they were on active duty at the time this accident occurred. The Koreans were outraged by all of this, and it brings back to them a great many other issues, including the fact that the headquarters of the 8th Army, which has been there since the Korean War, are located right in the center of one of the biggest and richest cities on the earth, Seoul—a city of twelve million people. This incident, and the fact that the South Koreans have so obviously been taken for granted by the American military, has led them to question a lot of other things. For example, do the American troops really defend them? South Korea is as large as and 25 times richer than North Korea. Is there really anything to be defended against when the major issues today are economic and economic integration and trying to avoid a sudden precipitous collapse of North Korea that would produce very severe and uncontrollable refugee flows? Moreover, South Korea, as it stands now, does not see how it can afford to integrate with North Korea. It has spent a lot of time studying East and West Germany and discovered how enormously costly that was to West Germany; they're not sure that they can do it. China also doesn't wish to see North Korea collapse at the present time. So they've all put subtle pressure on North Korea to begin to come in from the cold.

BONPANE: But U.S. belligerence goes way back. In April of 1997, Defense Secretary William Cohen said that the U.S. intended to keep forces stationed in Korea even if the two Koreas united.

JOHNSON: In that context, many South Koreans are starting to say, "Are the Americans an anachronism? They only seem to think in terms of cruise missiles and carrier task forces. We don't see the State Department. We don't see American civilians anymore. Maybe we don't need them any longer."

BONPANE: The young Koreans I talk to just speak of reunification.

JOHNSON: Yes, and they're no longer afraid of North Korea. South Korea has developed tremendous confidence in the way it's recovered from the 1997 economic crisis, for which it believes that the United States through the International Monetary Fund was largely responsible. I think their feeling today is that the time has passed for these old Cold War structures and that they're tired of being lectured to by American military officers.

BONPANE: Dr. Johnson, I have a quote from you concerning nuclear proliferation. You argue that until the Indian nuclear tests of May, 1998, in addition to Britain, France, China and Russia, proliferation had already occurred in Israel, Pakistan, and South Africa; and that South Korea, Japan, Sweden, Brazil, Argentina, Algeria and Taiwan had technologically proliferated without testing. The U.S. doctrine of nonproliferation also ignores the fact that there is something odd about the principle that permits some nations to have nuclear weapons but not others and that the United States has only been minimally willing to reduce its own monstrously large nuclear strike force.

JOHNSON: Well, we've had numerous Americans who have come out and said there was no conceivable reason for the United States to maintain this incredible, overwhelming nuclear force. Now we even have civilian militarists in our government plotting ways in which they might conceivably use these weapons.

BONPANE: If we're going to support preemptive strikes, we're going to give the word to India that it can attack Pakistan, or that China can attack Taiwan, and Russia can attack Chechnya. The message is clear. I see it as sociopathic.

JOHNSON: I agree with you, but moreover it would seem to me that the probable contradiction today between American policy with Iraq and American policy towards North Korea strongly suggests that this country is a bully. Iraq has already said in effect, "we should not have confronted the United States until we had weapons of mass destruction. The problem is we don't have any. If we did, we could

186

probably deter them."

BONPANE: Dr. Johnson, when you use the word "blowback," I can't help but think of it in terms of the Palestinian-Israeli conflict at this time. Can people get a handle on that relationship in terms of "blowback" after so much oppression since 1948?

JOHNSON: "Blowback" is a cynical term invented by the Central Intelligence Agency to refer to possible, unintended consequences of covert operations—of operations that were kept secret from the American public—and therefore, when the blowback comes, the American public is not able to put it into any context. They regard themselves, as they did on 9-11, as innocent bystanders. In some ways, the blowback in the Middle East today started at least 50 years ago with the first-ever use of the Central Intelligence Agency to overthrow, secretly, an elected government. This was the government of Iran—the government of Mohammed Mossadegh—and the CIA did so in conjunction with the British, because the British were irritated that Mr. Mossadegh wanted more profits from the Anglo-Iranian Oil Company to remain in Iran rather than their going to Britain. The British government was a large shareholder in that company, which later became British Petroleum. That set into motion a set of events that brought to power the Shah and an extremely right wing and repressive regime in Iran, resulting in 1979 in the overthrow of the Shah and the establishment of a fundamentalist Islamic regime under Ayatollah Khomeini. More seriously, the two main pillars of American policy in the Persian Gulf were authoritarian governments that were pro-American client states—Iran and Saudi Arabia—and one of those pillars fell away with the Revolution of 1979. Also, in that same year, as President Carter's National Security Advisor Zbigniew Brzezinski has since acknowledged, we began to support the unrest against the pro-Soviet government in Afghanistan. In December of 1979, the Soviet Union invaded Afghanistan. We then set up—again covertly—around the world an effort to bring in so-called "freedom fighters," *Mujahideen* (radical Muslims), to fight against the Soviet invaders. This was successful. It was paid for by us, armed by us, and it ultimately defeated the Soviet Union. It left Afghanistan in a terrible mess that we simply withdrew from, allowing the country to descend into an unbelievably destructive civil war. This of course came back to haunt us in 2001, on 9-11. But the other element in all of this, ironically, is that after that the Ayatollah Khomeini came to power in Iran, we decided to support his

187

then sworn enemy, namely "the tyrant" Saddam Hussein, who also came to power in 1979 in Iraq, and we encouraged a war between Iran and Iraq that was unbelievably bloody.

BONPANE: Henry Kissinger said, "Let them kill each other."

JOHNSON: Yes, and it lasted from 1980 until 1988. In 1982, when it began to look like the Iranians might actually defeat the Iraqis, we began covertly to supply Iraq—that is, Saddam Hussein—with intelligence, arms, and even the basic raw materials for the chemical weapons with which, as President Bush likes to say, he later gassed his own people. This is blowback. The Americans were not privy to any of this—not the American public or the Congress. It was all kept secret, and the blowback, the unintended consequences, included New York City on September 11, 2001. But the current administration wants to characterize the attackers of 9-11 as "evildoers," as a sort of evil force of nature, rather than asking, "What were their motives?" Because if you did start to ask about their motives and talk about what happened in Afghanistan over the last 20 years, as the United States and the Soviet Union covertly fought over the place, you would implicate some very high-ranking members of our current government who were responsible for our policies in Afghanistan—including the current Secretary of State, who was Chairman of the Joint Chiefs of Staff at the time, and the Vice President, who was Secretary of Defense, and Mr. Wolfowitz and Mr. Armitage.

You raised the Palestinian-Israeli issue. Let me just say a word here. After 9-11, I believe it was necessary to alter our foreign policy in light of new information. There were three things we should have done, and if we had done them, I believe the problem of terrorism would very likely have been at least controlled. First, we should have withdrawn the American troops that had been based in Saudi Arabia since 1991. They are seen by Saudi Arabians as being there to protect a repressive feudal government. The people regard this intrusion as a sacrilege, in that infidels are being used to defend a regime which has at least formally pledged to defend the most sacred sites in Islam, at Mecca and Medina.

BONPANE: And this has given rise to Osama Bin Laden and people like him.

JOHNSON: Precisely. So that was the first thing we should have done: withdraw American forces from Saudi Arabia. Secondly, we should have recognized that the most inflammatory issue in the Middle East is the feeling that the United States is not even-handed in the

Arab-Israeli conflict. We arm Israel, a country about the size of Hong Kong. We should have said, "As a matter of national policy, America is committed to, and would sign a treaty to guarantee, Israeli sovereignty and integrity. But we do not intend to support Zionist imperialism or any idea of a greater Israel. Therefore, our policy is that we are going to suspend aid to Israel until West Bank settlements are withdrawn and Israel quits making 'Bantustans' and apartheid-like enclaves for the miserable Palestinians."

The third thing we should have done was instantaneously to have begun in this country a program of fuel conservation. This could quite easily have reduced oil imports from Saudi Arabia and made ourselves free from our dependence on Persian Gulf oil. The problem, of course, is that we have done precisely the opposite on all three of these things. And therefore, the Central Intelligence Agency is utterly accurate when it says to Congress that we are in greater danger today from foreign terrorist attacks than we were on 9-11.

BONPANE: You know, it seems to me, Dr. Johnson, that practically every case we mentioned today relates to the lack of humanism. For example, I read in *The Independent* from Britain that seven million North Koreans are facing starvation. Can't we look at the situation this way rather than simply think in terms of weapons?

JOHNSON: Instead, there's going to be more blowback. If you should survive these next few months as an Iraqi or a North Korean, you're not going to have any doubt in your mind about who is the enemy. And you're also going to believe, as our Department of Defense has been talking about for the last 10 years, that our military is so overwhelmingly powerful today, no one will ever dare face us on the battlefield in a formal contest of arms. So what is now recommended, in a wonderful bit of Pentagon jargon, is "asymmetric warfare." This means, attack us where we're vulnerable, where we're weak, and that turns into the definition of terrorism that I used in *Blowback*: attacks on the innocent in order to draw attention to the sins of the invulnerable. The invulnerable, as we know, are people like our President and the Vice-President.

Blowback was written as a warning and was published in the spring of 2000. In it, I say, and strongly believe, many Americans are going to be surprised by the harvest of hostility from secret adventures we undertook throughout the Cold War and the first decade after the Cold War. The book I'm working on now, I'm sorry to say, is more of a diagnosis or even an autopsy. Militarism and imperialism are now so deeply advanced in the United States that it is quite hard to envision the circumstances under

189

which it could be reversed. The Department of Defense is today an Orwellian joke. It's not the Department of Defense; it's an alternative government on the south bank of the Potomac River with enormous resources. It plays a tremendous economic role in the United States, being the world's largest seller of munitions and weapons. Contrary to the Constitution, 40 percent of the defense budget is secret, just as is the entire intelligence budget. The Constitution says quite explicitly that the American public should have an accurate accounting of how its tax monies are spent. That is one thing that no American will ever get today. Some people would say I'm being alarmist. I'd have to say, if I'm wrong, you're going to forgive me. You're going to be so pleased that I was wrong.

BONPANE: Dr. Johnson, there's no thought in my mind that you're being alarmist. I think militarism is destroying the United States. I think it's destroying Israel and has a potential of destroying the world.

JOHNSON: I agree with you.

BONPANE: I think one thing we can be happy about is that we do have a strong peace movement. We have to do what Mr. Nixon referred to in his memoirs when he saw a half-million people in the streets and realized that the rape of Indochina was over.

JOHNSON: In this context, I would also recommend that people read the memoirs of Daniel Ellsberg. It is an almost unbelievable tale of how a genuine insider—a military officer with combat experience in Vietnam, a defense intellectual at the RAND Corporation, a Ph.D. in Economics from Harvard—came to a kind of revelation leading up to his decision in 1969 to stop lying and expose the truth.

BONPANE: Indeed, he said that it was the contempt he saw on our part for the people of Indochina, and the contempt he saw for the people in the United States military as well, it was these two contempts that drove him to release his material, to feel he had a mandate to let people know what was going on.

JOHNSON: Yes, the Americans have been warned. Our first President, Washington, in his farewell address, and Eisenhower, in his farewell address, both spoke of the enormous dangers to liberty of overly large standing armies. That, to me, is the problem of today. I have no doubt that we may be a new Roman Empire and that we can probably even enforce our empire through military power, but the certain unintended consequence of doing that is tyranny at home.

BONPANE: Of course, and as Eisenhower also said, "Every weapon produced is a theft from the poor." Here we are at a time where we are incapable of meeting the needs of the people of the United States.

190

Forty-one million people in our country lack health insurance. And the deficit—we've gone from a $231 billion surplus to an estimated $159 billion deficit over 2002.

JOHNSON: But that's caused by militarism.

BONPANE: The last phase of every civilization has been militarism—whether it has been Rome or Greece or England or Spain or the Aztecs or the Mayans—it's incredible that that's usually the swan song of each civilization.

JOHNSON: And just in our own lifetime, we've actually seen the disappearance of the Soviet Union. The Soviet Union fell apart because of imperial overstretch, ideologically driven errors in its domestic economy, and an inability to reform. I personally see the United States starting to tread in the same path as its erstwhile competitor during the Cold War.

BONPANE: I think its military spending helped it to crash and I do believe that the Cold War actually started with Hiroshima in 1945 and was confirmed at Nagasaki. These led the Soviet Union to determine that it had to do something and wasted its whole legacy on arms, and because of that we are now following a similar path. I hope that we can have a voice of reason in this, and I think that certainly you have been one such voice.

JOHNSON: Thank you.

BONPANE: I just hope that your voice is heard more and more throughout the world because it is so important that we turn this around. The one exciting thing to me is that, since 9-11, we have been forming a coalition for world peace internationally.

JOHNSON: I totally agree with you, and think that one of the few optimistic things in the last few years has been that fantastic coalition of people that first came together in Seattle in November of 1999 to resist what was called it "globalization" but was clearly the attempt to forcibly organize defenseless economies around the world in ways favorable to the U.S. I hope that this coalition will continue and grow, but I remain disturbed by the extreme weakness of our so-called newspapers. They are basically propaganda agencies that continuously give a different spin to these things. I hope the peace movement will succeed, but the thing that impresses me in a work such as Ellsberg's is the degree to which the separation between the state and society is now so great.

BONPANE: That is why I think we have to go to the streets. My son was jailed in Seattle at the time you speak of and we are going to increase the number of people out there. It seems that people realize that we're at a point where we can't depend on the government and must make our will known in the streets.

Reverend James Lawson

April 6, 2003

BONPANE: Hello, this is Blase Bonpane with *World Focus*. I am just very privileged today to have here, in studio, one of the most prominent clergymen in our country and his prominence is related to the Fruits of the Spirit, to peace and justice, joy and love, and endurance and sheer goodness. The Reverend James Lawson spent a year in federal prison for refusing to serve in the Korean War. He studied Gandhian nonviolence in India and returned to the United States to become a mentor of nonviolence to Dr. Martin Luther King, who considered him the greatest teacher of nonviolence in the world. It was the Reverend Lawson who gave the non violence training to people who sat in at the lunch counters. When Dr. King came to Memphis to support the strike of the sanitation workers, James Lawson was pastor of the United Methodist Church there. It was on this occasion, April 4, 1968 that King was assassinated. Today is Dr. King's birthday. He would be 74 years old today. How much he did in so few years and there's so much to talk about. It's just a pleasure to be here. Not only that, but I also consider Reverend James Lawson as a very dear friend. Welcome, Reverend Lawson.

LAWSON: Thank you, Blase.

BONPANE: It's a joy to have you here on this day. So many thoughts about Reverend King on this particular day. But we're in the present and we want to think about what Dr. King might be doing if he were here with us at this time in 2003.

LAWSON: Well, that's a big question, Blase. Of course I, as something of a historian of the past 40 or 50 years, would have to say that had King not been assassinated, I maintain that society would be a vastly superior society for ordinary people. The assassinations of the 1960s changed this country forever. That's why those assassinations are not talked about and why they are fundamentally covered up by the media, by the government, and with many ordinary people who cooperated with

193

that cover-up. The assassination of the 1960s put a massive burden upon the emerging movement for justice, liberty and equality for all that was moving rather rapidly all through the 1960s. It deprived us of the major voices in many ways for the struggle and it deprived us of the people who could have helped us move to the next level of struggle.

BONPANE: James, you are very familiar by the work by Mr. Pepper where he brings out the concept of a conspiracy to kill king. Would you explain that?

LAWSON: Well, Bill Pepper, of course, human rights lawyer now working out of New York, spent nearly 20 years examining the scene, became James Earl Ray's lawyer in the last years, and basically put his reputation and money on the line to continue investigation of it behind the scenes. I participated with him in various ways. I think that that investigation has proved beyond a reason of a doubt that James Earl Ray did not kill Dr. King. He was killed, in fact, by a Memphis policeman, and the planners locally included at least one businessman in the community, the Memphis police department, probably also the CIA or the Military Intelligence, or the FBI, or all three of them. William Pepper's book *Orders to Kill: The Truth About the Assassination of Dr. Martin Luther King Jr.* is a book that's now both a hardcover edition and a paperback edition. Not a single major national publication has done a single review of that book. So fierce is the silence that it cannot even be discussed. So fierce is, in fact, this American defect in our character of denial of the past, denial of racism, denial of the annihilation of Native Americans in the millions, denial of slavery, denials of sexism, denial of economic injustice as a part of the economy. This is not based, as George Will and others try to pretend, on the lack of character of the poor, or the homeless or the hungry, but based on the economy. The economy produces the economic injustice of poverty.

BONPANE: Jim, you may have not gotten the media to review this book, but you got the Congress to accept the thesis of this book.

LAWSON: The Congress, in fact the Congress report in the early 70s, declared that it was a conspiracy to kill Dr. Martin Luther King Jr. Now they ran away from doing any questioning on what that conspiracy was, or who might be the people involved in it, or the agencies involved in it. They raised no questions about how to unpack that conspiracy, but they did announce in their report that's still available, that the death of Dr. Martin Luther King Jr.—I sometimes call it a crucifixion of Dr. Martin Luther King Jr.—indeed was a conspiracy.

194

BONPANE: I think that's a tremendous achievement. Now, let's see his words for today. He speaks for us today. And let's presume he's speaking to us about Iraq. He says, "A time comes when silence is betrayal. That time has come for us."

LAWSON: Yes, that speech was made April 4, 1967 at the Riverside Church in New York City. Exactly one year after that he was assassinated in April 4, 1968 in Memphis, Tennessee. He was calling for the breaking of the silence on the part of the religions of America concerning the Vietnam War. Now, I want to point out one of the flaws in some of the reports on Martin King. Martin King had not been silent on Vietnam. He spoke about it often. And I spoke frequently about Vietnam in the workshops and the training opportunities. I spoke all the time about the Cold War and war and American foreign policy in Angola and Mozambique. Also, he spoke in many of his major speeches before that. As early as 1965 as an example, Martin was sending different people, different staff from the SCLC, to peace gatherings. His wife was representing him in peace gatherings. He was invited by the International Fellowship of Reconciliation to go to Southeast Asia and spend a month looking for himself with another group of clergy. He could not go. He felt that he could not at that time, as Martin Luther King, as the symbol of our struggle, he could not at that time go. What he did, however, was call me and ask me to take his place. He asked the International Fellowship of Reconciliation, "Could the Reverend James Lawson, a member of my staff, go in my stead?" So I, at his behest, did drop everything and go to Southeast Asia for six weeks in July and August of 1965, where we toured and saw for ourselves what was going on and made conclusions. I reported what I saw and what I had concluded and what we had concluded to Dr. Martin King.

BONPANE: That's why what he says in his speech is so exceptionally accurate about the role of the National Liberation Front and the role of Ho and what Ho had said. And he had got it from you.

LAWSON: Exactly. Historical. The historical base in that speech—and I had reread it here a few years ago—is really astonishing. One of the best views you could get. In fact, if anyone wants to read about the Vietnam War, and get in a summary why it was the wrong war, I suggest that they read that speech at times to break the silence, because the historical piece is there. Also, Iraq is there, and I'll tell you how. It's there because he said to that packed church of all kinds of people—standing room only church gathering—he said that "If we cannot have a revolution of values in America, this time we're protesting Vietnam,

195

but next time we'll be protesting South Africa or Mozambique or—"

BONPANE: Venezuela.

LAWSON: Venezuela. Or El Salvador.

BONPANE: Peru.

LAWSON: In other words, he saw an important point that I maintain, that none of us who are critical of American foreign policy really have seen. And that is the war violence system in the United States is the enemy of the people of the United States. It is what fuels President Bush Administration in its push for war. It is a huge military apparatus. Four hundred billion dollar annual budget, and this excludes the money in the CIA and in military intelligence, and in covert activities. It excludes all of that. It excludes international aid that, for an example, will supply arms to Israel or Venezuela or Colombia, and so for and so on. In other words, this is just the top part of the iceberg, the $400 billion dollars.

BONPANE: Jim, he was trying to help us connect the dots. Forty-one million Americans lack health care now, up from 35 million a decade ago. Thirty-two million Americans live in poverty. Up more than 8 million from 25 years ago. Thirteen million children in the U.S. live in families without an adequate supply of food. 9.6 million Americans are without jobs. We've gone from $2.6 billion dollar budget surplus to an estimated $150 billion dollar deficit. All of this is war related, and I think that Dr. King was telling us years ago and it is equally true today.

LAWSON: Exactly.

BONPANE: So here we are now. King said in regard to Vietnam, he said, "There is at the outset, a very obvious, and almost vassal connection between the war in Vietnam, and the struggle I and others have been waging here in America. A few years ago, there was a shining moment in the struggle. It seemed as if there was a real promise of hope for the poor—both black and white—through the poverty program. There were experiments, hopes, new beginnings. Then came the buildup in Vietnam, and I watched the program broken and eviscerated as if it were some idle political plaything of a society gone mad on war."

LAWSON: Yes, and that "shining moment" he's talking about, is a period in about 1963-1965 in that period. There was a period of 18 to 24 months when the Congress passed Head Start Program, Medicare, Medicaid, money for public education, the Civil Rights Bill of 1964, the Voting Rights Bill of 1965, executive orders for public accommodations, so that Americans could travel wherever they wanted to without the resistance of racism and apartheid, and so forth. There were bills that tried to clear the air in terms of immigration, to desegregate immigration. A wide range of bills that came through Congress that were aimed at lifting the quality of life for all Americans. Now why is that so relevant? Because George Bush, with Republicans and Democrats alike, today remains in tune with the notion that those measures should be eviscerated, destroyed, irradiated, and the funds used for the $200 billion dollar cost of the war against Iraq.

BONPANE: Militarism is destroying the United States of America. He says here, "I knew that America would never invest the necessary funds or energies in rehabilitation of its poor, so long as ventures like Vietnam continue to draw men and skills and money in some demonic, destructive suction tube."

LAWSON: Exactly. And I want to add to that that the fact that war and violence in the United States are profitable enterprises. These are enterprises on the stock market. These are enterprises where a variety of people of wealth continue to get high dividends from the public dollar. From my tax dollar. From your tax dollar.

BONPANE: Can't we tell them, Jim, that they can't take it with them? Wouldn't that be nice on a Sunday?

LAWSON: Well, I have and you have, Blase, I'm sure. But the point is that as long as the Congress and the presidents are geared towards the notion that war is profit, then of course, we have this war machinery that dominates the domestic scene and will dominate it. And it's not a question of whether Saddam or Iraq are mean and bitter. Well, we have a lot of mean and bitter people in Washington today that govern our country.

BONPANE: We've supported them.

LAWSON: So that's not the issue. The issue is not human sin. There's enough human sin that all of us are implicated by it. But the point is that we have absolutely no business waging war against colored nations who, for hundreds of years, been the nations under the heel of Western European states. In other words, colonialism has been the hallmark of the last 500 years. Iraq has not come out of colonialism yet.

BONPANE: Martin Luther King says here, "Perhaps the more tragic recognition of reality took place when it became clear to me that the war was doing far more devastating the hopes of the poor at home. It was sending their sons and brothers and their husbands to fight and die in extraordinarily high proportions relative to the population." That applies right now.

LAWSON: Absolutely. In fact one of my good friends and I were in conversations a couple of weeks ago. He is now a priest in northeastern New Mexico, a very impoverished part of our country. The thing he said that surprised him—he's been there six months maybe at the most now—the thing that surprised him was the extent to which in that impoverished area in those villages, the army, navy and air force recruiters are everywhere recruiting the poor to go into the "voluntary" army. And recruiting them on the basis that "this will get you out of poverty. We'll give you an education." In other words, "the schools there can't give you an education, a leg up and an opportunity, but we'll give you an opportunity. Travel the world; we'll give you education. We'll make access to democracy and liberty for you available." So that's the pitch. So, you decrease the money in public education; decrease, therefore giving every child a world-class education, while you increase the military budgets. Then you go into those urban and rural areas of poverty and you recruit those young people, those children of ours for the purpose of war. I shall never forget Vietnam. One of the reasons I'll never forget it is that I was a pastor at the time in Centenary United Methodist Church, and I had three to five young men, most of them taken out of college—black young men taken out of college in Vietnam—during those years. And the death ratio in Memphis was 50 percent white, 50 percent black.

BONPANE: Wow, and no relationship, no co-relation to the percentages of people?

LAWSON: This was evident in any number of urban areas. Those statistics were available back then and are more than available now.

BONPANE: Jim, the No Child Left Behind Act, insists every child's name be given, every address of every child in high school be given, every phone number be given to the military recruiters. And they are recruited day and night, especially in the poorer areas of this country.

LAWSON: Exactly. And this "No Child Left Behind" is a lie.

BONPANE: Of course it's a lie.

LAWSON: It's right out of the annals of Nazi Germany.

BONPANE: Jim, we have a contradictory administration. All of the appointments are contradictory of what they are supposed to do. First of all, the non-election of the president is contradictory. Every appointment made by the president has been contradictory. They assigned someone to environment who's opposed to the environment; they assigned someone to defense who's a warmonger. All of this has been contradictory. I would love to ask the President to do ask what Mr. Nixon was good enough to do. He resigned and that was a tremendous achievement. And then the Vice President could resign, and maybe we could also put together a new government. I'd like to quote once more from King here and am asking for your comment. He says, "They asked if our own nation wasn't using massive doses of violence to solve its problems, to bring about the changes it wanted. Their question hit home and I knew I would never again raise my voice against the oppressed in the ghettos without having first spoken clearly to the greatest purveyor of violence in the world today—my own government."

LAWSON: Yes, I think it stands clear today that Martin King said that. I have said in the 60s the United States government is the number one enemy of peace and justice in the United States and in the world. I say it somewhat differently today, but it seems to me that all government in the United States has subverted their responsibility to the people to the war aim—the covert Pentagon, CIA, State Department, Congress, the White House—these institutions no longer serve democracy. They serve injustice. I can never forget in the early 1960s discovering in the press that American helicopters were in Mozambique and Angola dropping our napalm on United Methodist sisters and brothers of mine, whose only crime was that they had decided that it was time for Portugal to give up those colonies and allow the people there to begin to govern and determine their own destiny. I had colleagues there in both Angola and Mozambique who did their studies in Europe and the United States where I met them in various student associations, and they were active in their efforts to organize their people for independence and for democracy. My government called all of them communists and then proceeded to loan Portugal the wherewithal, so that today even as we speak, Mozambique is destitute. A consequence then of a further effort by Reagan and Jesse Helms to support the apartheid government and to use the apartheid government as a surrogate army in stopping independence movements north of them, Mozambique continues to be one of the countries where a high percentage of mines are scattered all over the jungles and everywhere. It has the highest per capita paraplegic population among the children in the world.

BONPANE: Jim, while you were observing that I was in Guatemala, which was being napalmed secret at the same time and I had to blow the whistle on that through the *Washington Post*. It's the same thing; these secret wars were going on. Now, Dr. King says, "If America's soul becomes totally poisoned, part of the autopsy must read Vietnam. It can never be saved so long as it destroys the deepest hopes of men

199

the world over." And then there's this book called *Killing Hope* by William Blum showing all the different examples of Mozambiques of the world and the Guatemalas of the world. How are we going to turn this around? We don't have change from the top and I want our listeners to think for a moment about the impact of the religious community in the abolition of slavery and in the coming of the civil rights movement, that the religious movement was there. It's sad to me, Jim, to think that oftentimes great publications, even publications like *The Nation* are horrified by the religious right as it is called, but they seem unaware of the impact of progressive religious people in our history such as Fr. Roy Bourgeois' work in Georgia in the School of the Americas Watch. I think that the most militant agents of change have been progressive religious people historically. And I think it's important for us to see that today.

LAWSON: Yes, I think we must acknowledge that all across this country, the major struggle for equality, liberty, and justice has come from the struggle of the American people, and that a variety of religious congregations and leaders have played a very large role in that. The abolitionist movement prior to 1860 was, of course, riddled with church-folk who opposed. Obviously the movement of the 50s and 60s, what I call sometimes the "King Movement," rather than the Civil Rights Movement or the "Freedom Movement," the church was our only institution where we could meet. The clergy were the freest people to give leadership to it. We did not depend for our income from a corporation or a factory, so that meant that we depended on our income from our own people. So consequently, we were the freest people to be able to provide leadership. And so much of the media, in my judgment, seems to forget that Jerry Falwell, James Kennedy and others, represent not the best of religion; they represent an ideological effort to manage and control religion around their basic white, and I'll say male, values.

BONPANE: Well, this is what has led to some 30 religious wars around the world today. Falwell is urging people to identify with the Likud Party in Israel, saying that this is going to lead to Armageddon, which is going to hasten the second coming of Christ, as if Christ needed Falwell to come back. He'll come back whenever he pleases. He doesn't depend on Jerry Falwell.

LAWSON: And of course, also that is only one way to think about the Christ returning. In my judgment, another way of looking at it spiritually is how Christ as the word of God, the word of life and love, returns in every human being who applies their life to the way of compassion and truth and hope in the world today.

BONPANE: Now we're getting somewhere when we look at it that way. I think we can see it more clearly. King said, "Could it be that they do not know that the Good News was meant for everyone? For communist and capitalist; for their children and ours; for black and white; for revolutionary and conservative? Have they forgotten that my ministry is in obedience to the one who loved his enemies so fully that he died for them? When, then, can I say to the Viet Cong or to Castro or to Mao as a faithful minister of this one? Can I threaten them with death or must I not share with them my life?"

LAWSON: Exactly, which means therefore, Blase, that today the Americans who are in silent numbers but increasing numbers, saying no to Iraq, saying no to hypocrisy of the present Congress and presidential administration, saying yes to the eradication of racism and poverty and hunger at home, but no to the violence. No to the war. No to the expending of millions of people being used to fight. Just imagine if we used simply half of those resources over a protracted period of time to eradicate poverty and hunger in the United States, to eradicate illiteracy, to build quality education and quality health care, think of what kind of progress this would mean for America and then for our world.

BONPANE: We could end world poverty just with the cost of militarism. And I think, Jim, we're going to have to give ourselves credit every now and then. For example, at the present time, we have the largest preemptive peace movement in history. This is all before the outbreak of hostilities. I think there is something going on that the media sometimes calls the "Vietnam Syndrome." What a poor word. A syndrome is an illness. This is a mutation in the thinking of people in terms of what is patriotism, what it is to care.

LAWSON: Let me just say to you, that in the 50s and 60s, I was appalled constantly at being questioned by reporters in Birmingham, Little Rock or Memphis or Nashville or elsewhere on what we were about. They had an appalling unawareness of the American people. Ignorant of American history. Unaware of what segregation, what apartheid had done to them and to our society.

BONPANE: No history.

LAWSON: No background, no knowledge. They may have had a degree from some place, but their questions were very limited.

BONPANE: And they remain that way.

LAWSON: And that's the media.

BONPANE: Yes, it's pathetic to hear them.

LAWSON: The media now more deliberately than 1960, I think, is geared to the notion of dumbing down the American people so that American people can be illiterate about themselves and the world.

BONPANE: Jim, King said, "We are called to speak for the weak, for the voiceless, for victims of our nation, and for those it calls "enemy," for no document from human hands can make these humans any less our brothers."

LAWSON: Exactly. Well that's just fundamental biblical understanding. We talk about Jerry Falwell's use of the bible. Well, Jerry Falwell for many years used the bible to beat up black people to indicate that it was for segregation. Now he is gung-ho trying to make the bible dictate to the nation that gay and lesbian people are somehow people outside of God's love, which is nonsense.

BONPANE: And they caused the attack on the twin towers?

LAWSON: The Americans need to wake up and read the bible for themselves and understand that the fundamental theme of the bible is what he has put his finger on. The Old Testament and New Testament alike insist that the well being of the nation is dependent on justice. The Book of Proverbs says, "The king establishes stability by justice." We're to keep our eyes on the widow, to the hungry. Jesus added the children very clearly, the stranger, the alien. By being concerned for their well-being, we best our concern for our well-being. Life cannot be gained by losing it in greed or in the highest possible standard living or as such a thing as financial security. Because as you said, "you can't take it with you anyway." Life is best gained as Gandhi said, as Albert Einstein said, as King said, as Pope John XXIII said, and a whole range of human beings across the centuries has said, life is made secure by losing one's life in the cause of building the community.

BONPANE: Jim, I think we're breaking through something because the international edition of *Time* magazine this week asked what the greatest threat to peace was in the world, and 72% of the people responded, the United States. Something's going on.

LAWSON: *Time* magazine asked what is the greatest threat to peace?

BONPANE: This is incredible. Yes. The United States. Yes. This is a tremendous breakthrough. This is like the breakthrough with the *L.A. Times* last Sunday when they covered that magnificent peace gathering.

LAWSON: This is incredible.

BONPANE: Yeah, something's happening, Jim. Something's going on. We're breaking in to the actual power media. Not every day, but it's really

202

amazing that this is transpiring at this time.

LAWSON: This is astonishing. That should be the news. That should be a major piece of news, actually.

BONPANE: It is.

LAWSON: No, but *Time* magazine. In the electronic media it's not.

BONPANE: Yeah, of course. The TV hasn't picked it up. But it's out there. It's very exciting that this has happened and of course, the numbers of people that showed up in Washington help us to remember the words of Mr. Nixon when he looked out his window and saw a half-million people in the streets and said he knew that the war was over. When you get a half-million people in the streets paying their own way to Washington, taking great sacrifices, in some case, either threatening or losing their job, to come out and put their body on the line.

LAWSON: We're well on our way to having a half-million here and a half-million in Chicago and a half-million in New York and a half-million in D.C. And hundreds of thousands all over the world. It has to happen.

BONPANE: Well, we've seen it in Italy. My God, in Florence, Italy; in England, Harold Pinter came out. He spoke at the House of Commons with the most damning speech against Tony Blair that has ever happened. He connected Tony Blair with Oliver Cromwell and he just lambasted him and said, "Well you know you're not representing the people of England, you're not representing our hopes, desires, anxieties," and Tony's going to have to get out of this thing or get out of government. That's where it's at.

LAWSON: I hope so. I hope so. I have real problems with the possibility, only with the point of view that we have the best president and the best Congress that money can buy. And that money is still available, so they may very well hang on because, you know, a nation's progress very often is not something swift and sure. It may take decades for it to slide downhill until enough people have seen it. But if 72 percent of the people said United States is the greatest threat to peace and all, it seems to me that what we and the people have to do is put millions of ourselves in the streets all across this country and it must become a protracted struggle. It can't be today and let it go for six weeks. We've got to pick up the pace in Los Angeles for the vigils that are going on now almost every day, the prayer sessions almost every day around the entire county and metropolitan area. We must pick that up, we must pick up the picket lines and the marches so that then we will deliver the word to Gray Davis and to Mayor Hahn and to our city councilmen, "It's time for you all to take leadership and go to

George Bush and the Congress in no uncertain term, and do it publicly and do it in an angry fashion, or at least a convicted fashion, that the money you are wasting on war and to tax cuts on the wealthy must be distributed across this country in an equitable fashion so that we can do the things that we must be able to do to help the people of our land.

BONPANE: That was our same suggestion at the massive rally in Los Angeles that we now continue on a daily basis. We cannot simply have this on occasion. This has to be daily. And Jim, as you know, the strange thing is that those old segregationists in the Senate and in the Congress at the time of the Civil Rights movement suddenly got religion and they decided to change their ways, not because they had changed up here any more than Senator Lott had, because they had changed their mind, but politically they had to change. So we don't care if these warmongers change, as St. Paul said, "in pretence or in truth," so long as they change.

LAWSON: Well, this is where Blase, you and I have a disagreement. Because I happen to think that Trent Lott has not really been transformed. He's changed his language in part, but he still calls himself a conservative, and by a conservative he does not mean, "I am for civil liberties and human rights. I want to preserve the best of our society." By conservative, he means, "We need to go back to some stage where white supremacy is the overt rule of the land."

BONPANE: That's why he said, "It caused all the trouble."

LAWSON: That's right. Changing segregation caused all the trouble in the land. Yes, exactly. So, George Bush has a lot of that stuff in him, mixed up as it may be. So it's my thesis that spiritually, racism is very much alive in the ideologies that pretend folk, like George Wills has said that, "our problem with race today is only that we have some dysfunctional black people." It's not economic, it's not social, it's not political, it's not the violence of capital punishment or the violence of jails and prisons of the criminal system in America. It's not the violence of the millions of adults who work every day and cannot earn enough to keep food on their tables or to care for their children, as they would like to care for them. This, in my judgment, is only a couple of degrees away from the 250 years of slavery, which was a national economic institution. The principle is still here. The people can work and they don't have to earn money. Another facet of that in my judgment is that George Bush wants to provide work through the defense industry rather than through education, health care, housing, transportation, affordable jobs.

BONPANE: Nothing is more damaging. If you think for a moment, Jim, just think about paying 37,000 troops for 50 years, what that does, you create all that money, say in the case of Korea. That many troops have been in Korea. They have been paid every time. All that money is created for not producing anything at all.

LAWSON: That the people can use.

BONPANE: Therefore, a $50,000 house is $500,000. Too much money is looking for each useful item. It has destroyed the economy.

LAWSON: And the $80 billion dollars was used to keep troops in Arab bases and Europe.

BONPANE: We have troops in over a hundred countries today. This is destroying us. It destroyed Rome and Greece and Great Britain, the King's army, the King's navy, as it destroyed Spain, as it destroyed the Aztecs and the Mayans, and we're in that same posture. Militarism is the last phase of any culture. It is destroying the United States. It is destroying Israel. It is destroying everything that it touches. It destroyed what there was in the effort to be a Union of Soviets. It didn't work because militarism ended their efforts to put a country together. It didn't happen and we're there again.

LAWSON: It seems to me that it has to be said that right now in the United States, the militarism is undermining all sorts of civil liberties. All sorts of due process on the part of the constitution. Ashcroft and Bush are fundamentally canceling the Constitution of the United States and doing it both by executive order but by behavior and the rest of it. Now, you and I are enemy combatants by the U.S. Patriot Act. They can declare any of us enemy combatants, arrest us, pick us up, put us in jail. We'll have no opportunities for lawyers. This is what they're already doing to the males from 25 or 30 Muslim countries, many of them citizens.

BONPANE: Jim, the Patriot Act was written before 9-11. They were simply waiting for an opportunity and occasion to put into place. It was their goal to destroy the Constitution from the beginning. That act was not written after 9-11. After 9-11, they said, "Ah, now is the time."

LAWSON: And, of course, also it should be said that a whole array of religious people in this society stand in the wings because they see this as steps towards making the United States a theocracy, an authoritarian society and a dictatorship similar to Iran, where the clergy are in charge, where Jesus is the flag, and so forth and so on. And the media seems to act as though they're not aware of this movement within the country to cancel out democracy. There is a similarity between it and the development of the Nazi party in Germany.

BONPANE: Germany was always talking about terrorism, and Jefferson was very much touched with the problem of a theocracy. He was seeing witch burners. He was seeing all sorts of people who wanted a sectarian state and that's why he insisted there should be no law regarding a religion. "What do they think as we test our latest weapons on them just as the Germans tested out new medicine and new torture in the concentration camps of Europe?

LAWSON: Exactly. I was reflecting on that this morning earlier because a part of the great need of the United States is to see American foreign policy, not from the point of view of the official line, the official party line out of the Pentagon, or D.C. or the Congress, but out of the point of view of the people who we are contending against. That's what we will not do. It is to me astonishing that George Bush can say, "They hate us," but in my travels abroad, I have found very few people who hate us. They are troubled by our policies towards them. Not by any kind of conception of hate, of being hateful of us. They are people of great compassion. I sat in a home of the Heider family in Bashra, Iraq in the year 2000. One of the bombs from the continued bombing that's going on landed in their street and killed their five-year-old boy, and wounded their two-year-old—or three-year-old—boy. A group of us Americans sat at their invitation and their living room as they talked to us about this. There were no traces of hate in that room. Mother, father, the surviving boy, grandparents, at least one uncle, and then a number of other friends on that street. The bomb landed on their street and several people were killed. They said, "We are puzzled. We don't hate you. We're puzzled by why you're bombing us."

BONPANE: It is amazing the greatness of people around the world.

LAWSON: Astonishing to me.

BONPANE: I found the same thing in Nicaragua, El Salvador—

LAWSON: Yes, astonishing.

BONPANE: In Guatemala, and in Iraq as well in Babylon, I was there, it has probably been totally destroyed.

LAWSON: And the truth of the matter is that most people in the world have compassion for one another and compassion for other people in the world.

BONPANE: Think about it, Jim, we've killed almost two million people in Iraq. Talking about one man as though there's one person who lived there. Organized crime has never been that sloppy.

LAWSON: No, has never been that sloppy. We killed three to five million people in Vietnam, and we mourn our 50,000. Well, if there is a God, Blase, as you well know, is that God only concerned with those 50,000 Americans?

BONPANE: No.

LAWSON: Let's eliminate the name "God," but let's say there's a life force that has produced us and brought us to this place. Is that life force that is in all the people of the world only concerned for American life?

BONPANE: No. We're into 19th century nationalistic thinking. We have to start planetary thinking. We live in a very small planet that is in grave danger of looking like Pluto or Mars or the moon. We are about to eliminate the life on this planet by virtue of militarism. The time has come to abolish the war system, to have an abolition movement of it. We have to create a peace system, which has actually been structured at the top. We have an excellent system of peace established through a charter of the United Nations. Now we at the base have to insist that that international system be put into place.

LAWSON: And we have an excellent basis for peace in the Declaration of Independence and the Constitution of the United States, which means we have a political task. We have to either raise up some new political parties or we have to elect some of the better people of society who have compassion and a zeal for liberty and justice. Not hypocrisy. Because I think that Rumsfeld and Bush are hypocrites of the worse order in the American scene. They grin at us and tell us that "we're for democracy and we're doing right by you," but they've got their whole lives organized around war. Well, war itself is the greatest crime against human rights.

BONPANE: These people are behaving as sociopaths. That is, that they have no concern for humanity. Humanity is what we need. This is going to save us if we reflect on the fact that we're talking about blowing the heads off of Iraqi children in the name of their oil company—that is our oil companies in our country—this is not acceptable. King said, "They watch as we poison their water, as we kill a million acres of their crops. They must weep as the bulldozers roar through their areas preparing to destroy the precious trees. They wander into hospitals with at least 20 casualties from American firepower for one 'Viet Cong' inflicted injury. So far, we may have killed a million of them, mostly children. They wander into the towns to see thousands of the children homeless, without clothes, running in packs on the streets like animals. They see the children degraded by our soldiers as they beg for food. They see the children selling their sisters to our soldiers, soliciting for their mothers."

LAWSON: Yes, exactly. And of course, part of the fatal flaw it seems to me in the United States is the notion that by doing evil things, you can create good. And it simply is not true. It is why King was a nonviolent person, and a nonviolent political figure, and a nonviolent pastor and preacher and a revolutionary; because it is only through nonviolent struggle that you can create a future that is hopeful for the human race. We in the United States should have learned from gang violence, from the ways of homicide and murder and rape and domestic violence in the United States, these things have not blessed us. These things have hurt us.

BONPANE: They're imitating our foreign policy.

LAWSON: So we ought to learn. We should learn from that and reverse it and insist that we must become a nonviolent society, a nonviolent culture.

BONPANE: King says: "Here is the true meaning of and value of compassion and nonviolence: when it helps us to see the enemy's point of view, to hear his questions, to know his assessment of ourselves. For from his view, we may indeed see the basic see the basic weaknesses of our own condition. And if we are mature, we may learn and grow and profit from the wisdom of brothers who are called the opposition." How we could learn from them? It's an extremely good point.

LAWSON: One of the things that we need to emphasize in these days as we celebrate the life of King—well two things—one of them is that we must celebrate the movement as well, because it is the struggle of the people that was about. But secondly, we ought to celebrate the fact that his religious insight is of greater importance to the United States than probably all of the religiosity that one can hear on the radio and television today. Far more important. That's not unusual, because obviously in a time of the biblical prophets, we have the book of Jeremiah. Jeremiah had a major popular preacher who was opposed to him by the name of Hananiah. But we don't have a book of Hananiah in the Bible. We have the book Jeremiah. Jeremiah insisted that there was a better way and the popular religion was not going to bring it about. It was only going to be through people repenting of violence and brokenness and economic injustice and restoring compassion and truth—what he called obedience to God—righteousness before God.

BONPANE: If we could only get that message, that we aren't going to accomplish this through sectarianism. We aren't going to accomplish it through psychotic fundamentalism. We're going to accomplish it through looking for the fruits. Jesus said, "By their fruits you shall know them." If we see the fruits of peace, patience, goodness, kindness, joy and love, we know we're on the right track. If we see hatred envy and greed of the leadership, we know that is where the evil is. We respect, in this fashion, all religions, because each of them have this at their base and here we are at this time trying to get this point across. It's not a sectarian message. It's not a nationalistic message. Because we can have a nationalistic fundamentalism, which is just as harmful as religious fundamentalism. I don't know how to thank you for being with us, Reverend James Lawson, because you are a continuation of Dr. King's mission, and you're with us today and we look upon you as a leader in the movement today for peace. I think that this is the greatest crisis in the history of the United States. We have to deal with the sickness in our government and make every attempt for our people to enter into the hopes, desires and anxieties of the rest of the world instead of looking at others as the enemy. And you're with us to make that happen.

LAWSON: Yes, I wholeheartedly concur, and personally I can do no other. I must be involved and try to continue to sow these seeds. And I hope and pray that our work through the Interfaith Community United for Justice and Peace, the Coalition for World Peace, and the Fellowship of Reconciliation, and the ACLU, we can indeed get the American people to the place where we say to our government, "Enough is enough. Now you come home and you begin to deal with these issues that are affecting the American people. Let's give the American people a new fresh burst of liberty, equality and justice for all.

BONPANE: This is Blase Bonpane. I've been speaking with the Reverend James Lawson. I'm extremely grateful to you, Reverend James Lawson for being the voice of the voiceless for so many years. And you're going to be that voice for many years ahead. God bless you and thank you so much for being here.

LAWSON: Thank you, Blase.

Jonathan Schell

July 6, 2003

BONPANE: Hello, this is Blase Bonpane with World Focus. I'm very honored today to have Jonathan Schell with us. He's the author of many books, including *Time of Illusion*, *The Fate of the Earth*, and *The Village of Ben Suc*. He's been a contributor to *The Nation*, *The New Yorker*, *Harper's*, *The Atlantic* and *Foreign Affairs*. He's taught at Wesley, Princeton and Emory Universities among others. He's currently living in New York where he's the Harold Willens Peace Fellow at The Nation Institute. Jonathan has just released the book, *The Unconquerable World: Power, Nonviolence and the Will of the People*. Jonathan, thank you so much for being with us today.

SCHELL: The pleasure is mine.

BONPANE: Jonathan, you speak of a war system and I found that very striking. Maybe you could tell our listeners what you mean by a war system.

SCHELL: Well, by the war system, I'm really referring to something that in a certain sense is something of the past. Let me explain what I mean. A war system really consists of a number of countries—five, six, ten, whatever it is—that are in proximity to one another and are jockeying for military power. Maybe they are allying sometime, fighting sometime, trying to balance one another sometime. Sometime there arises in their midst someone who seeks hegemony. But really, it's a system of many powers, and a characteristic of it really is that they engage in competition, that is an arms race. Insofar as you can create safety in a war system through a balance of power, but when that gets upset, the whole thing can plunge into horror as happened in 1914 in the first World War. The reason I refer to that as something, which in a certain sense has sunk in the past, is that at that top level of international affairs where those great powers were jockeying with one another; the nuclear weapon came, which was invented in 1945 and intervened and, in a way, put a stop to the kind of world war that has always been a danger and, in fact, twice a feature of the war system.

So the war system, as once existed, is really no longer in existence. We have something that is really quite different. First, in the Cold War, now to something quite different right now that we need to analyze really quite carefully.

BONPANE: Well, in this type of system, even in what we have today, don't we see something that has all the components of a cult? A great leader who cannot be disobeyed, the question of various lies being given as the truth, and those who are fighting the war not free to leave, even under threats of death? Isn't this a cult-type of situation?

SCHELL: Well, I think in any given country that can arise. I was just reading in *The Nation* magazine that I write for, a wonderful piece by John Dower on the rise of militarism in Japan in the 1930s. He points out the very many striking resemblances between that transformation of Japan and what he fears is happening in the United States. One of those was definitely a kind of military expansionism that went hand in hand with the domestic-political transformation. That was all fuelled by a very intense nationalism. And once they had gone to war, the patriotic, or nationalistic, sentiments rose very high and really prevented, or cancelled out, any possibility of dissent; and once you cancel out that possibility, then of course, you have the situation that you have mentioned before. As Dower points out, back in Japan at that time, they had an actually functioning emperor, so named, so imperialism was a rather natural thing, or more natural for them than today. Whereas today, here in the United States, I think we have a kind of bid for empire, but it's not so called. So there still is something in the United States that resists that. But we do seem to be headed in the direction of a kind of unitary system of public opinion that certainly can develop cult-like aspects.

BONPANE: You mentioned the analysis of Carl von Clausewitz who lived from 1780 to 1831. He had an analysis of war and seemed to have some hope that it would not always be an extension of politics by other means. Do you feel that Clausewitz saw the futility of the war system?

SCHELL: I don't think he did actually. The usefulness of Clausewitz from my point of view was that he was a dazzling thinker and he gave to me what was the most careful and sound analysis of what war is—that is when I speak of war I mean conventional war—and what a war system is. How victory and defeat are arrived at, what victory and defeat are, and how you get either one. The usefulness of that for me was precisely not because it described the world of today but because it served as a benchmark from which to measure the distance from which we've

211

traveled in the nuclear age.

BONPANE: Well, in terms of Clausewitz, you mentioned on page 18 that the "victor or his proconsul has taken up residency in the capital of the defeated nation," and naturally when I read of this I'm thinking of Iraq. "He issues an order. Do the defeated people obey? Do they do his will? Perhaps he had thought he had won the victory when the enemy forces dissolve, but now it turns out, according to Clausewitz, that the decision made by civilians, far from the field of battle, will determine whether he really was victorious after all, for the war cannot be considered to have ended so long as the enemy's will has not been broken." Does this not have a ring to it today?

SCHELL: Yes, indeed it does. And you know, Clausewitz, notwithstanding what I just said about his power to define a war about that period or a given period, he was such a deep thinker and such a careful analyst, that when he tackled the question of when victory and defeat really occur, he saw into certain dilemmas that were only marginal in his time, but have appeared in ours. And one of those was the peculiar question of what it is that really constitutes defeat. In other words, when is a country defeated and when does the country attacking it know that it has been defeated? Now, you know, the simple answer is that when you defeat the other army in the field of battle and they run away, then you've won. But what Clausewitz saw was that there was another kind of power in the background that was really the object of military campaign, and that is to say that if the opposing army was scattered and ran, but then you went into the capital of the supposedly-defeated country and you were still resisted by the population there, then had you really won? And he gave the example of Napoleon marching into Russia, but finding that the Russians wouldn't play ball with him, but eventually he had to withdraw and was defeated. So, the point that he saw, although he didn't go into it very deeply because historical circumstances hadn't provided the events for that except in a few cases, was that this question of whether defeat occurs is a rather mysterious business. It doesn't just depend on the number of forces you have and it doesn't depend either on the battles you win. There's something else beyond that, underneath that, something that is not of a strictly military character.

BONPANE: Seems to me that when Clausewitz, as you mentioned, spoke of Russia in 1812 where he won every battle on the way to Moscow, and then we could ask the question, "Weren't the Russians beaten?" And then, in fact, as all the readers of Tolstoy's War and Peace know,

212

the will of Russia was intact. It was Napoleon who was on his way to ruin. So these are in a way Pyrrhic victories.

SCHELL: Yeah, that's exactly what they were. For instance, when Napoleon defeated Clausewitz's own Prussia in 1806, well, Prussia was well and truly defeated in classical style and had to submit to losing half of their country being ruled by Napoleon for a while. But in Russia, it was otherwise, and it turned out that that experience in Russia as we can read about in *War and Peace* as I suggest there, was really a harbinger of the future. Just to give you an example, I cut my teeth as a reporter in Vietnam way back in the late 1960s. And what I witnessed day in and day out was the American forces winning just about every battle. I think this is not really appreciated, because of the staggering firepower that the U.S. had, that we were really the victors in every battle. And yet we lost the war.

BONPANE: Yes, that seems to be the point that Clausewitz was making in regard to Napoleon in Russia. So there does seem to be some continuity there and it does concern us that in this particular moment of history we are in a level of militarism greater than at any other time in history. Now, on the very positive side, we spoke of a war system, there is also the very beginnings of a peace system, which started even prior to World War I, and then became institutionalized through the League after World War I and was defeated by our own Senate. Now why would the Senate destroy the League of Nations?

SCHELL: Well, to oversimplify, they feared it would be an abridgment of American sovereignty. They were not ready to give up the degree of power to an international organization that really would have been necessary to make the League of Nations function. They were also afraid of getting dragged into all kinds of wars around the world that other nations would pull us into. I think that was nevertheless, even though the League of Nations failed, I think it was a real turning point in people's consciousness about war. Now of course it failed, and in a sense the United Nations too failed in its larger purpose in bringing overall peace in the world as we can see today. Nevertheless, I think that back in 1919, there was a sort of rebellion against war that was deeper than there had been before. I mean, war has always been hated by those who were killed, their family, friends, and children and so forth. That's always been understood to be a scourge and peace has always been a dream. But there was a kind of a feeling that was very widespread throughout the world that with eight or nine million people killed in the First World War, that this was really intolerable. I think

213

that feeling, even though it hasn't been given effect, has remained in the world as a factor, and is something that can rise up again.

BONPANE: Well, we saw it blossom on February 15 when tens of millions of people came out in a coordinated fashion—in a planetary fashion—not simply to oppose any aggression against Iraq, but it seemed quite clear that they were opposing the whole concept of war itself. So I think that impetus that began with the League and continued with the formation of the United Nations is still with us. In fact, it seems to be reaching a higher level.

SCHELL: Well it is, and what was so striking and so encouraging about February 15 was that this wasn't a deed of government. It was a deed of just people spontaneously reacting throughout the world.

BONPANE: I think it's important for our listeners to know that today we're speaking with Jonathan Schell, who has written another magnificent book. This one is called: *The Unconquerable World: Power, Nonviolence, and the Will of the People.* The thought here in the title itself is that all the great empires never conquered the planet. On the contrary, they disintegrated from the early days of the Romans and Greeks, all the way through to the present here. And I think we can read between the lines here that if we don't want to disintegrate ourselves, we had better take a new look at what we're doing. That's what I get out of it.

SCHELL: Well that's what I put into it, if I may say so.

BONPANE: I thought that's where you were going. It's the kind of book that many people defining a work of art say, "I understand it. I'm in communion with the artist. I couldn't have done it but I understand what he or she was doing, and I wish I had done it myself." And that's the feeling I had in reading your book because there's so many of these points of extreme importance, not the least of which is the development of a movement of nonviolence from the base of the community. We all studied this in our history books in the first and second grade about the great nonviolent civil disobedience that was called the "Boston Tea Party." Now we're seeing similar actions. Internationally, for example, we just saw the Riverside Ploughshares Group, a group who made a symbolic action in the spirit of the Tea Party. They got on board the *U.S.S. Philippine Sea*, poured their blood on a missile silo, and hit it with hammers, not doing any real damage, but just making their point, and they're facing very serious charges. This type of symbolic act I think speaks to us today. Are you in touch with this type of action?

SCHELL: Yes, indeed I have the highest respect for those people and the

214

Ploughshares group. These are religious people. I think they are Christians. I'm not sure if every one is a Christian, but I think its very much Christian in inspiration. Biblical in inspiration—beating swords into ploughshares. These are people who have taken into heart the inconceivable fact of the nuclear age, namely that we do threaten to kill really hundreds of millions of people—in fact everybody on earth—and who have taken that to heart and decided to live a life that is appropriate to that circumstance, which to them because they are courageous means acts of civil disobedience. By the way, that case you just mentioned, they've been accused of charges with very long prison sentences. Twenty years and such—I'm not sure if that is the correct figure or not—but very draconian prison sentences. Some of these are nuns. For those of us who haven't quite had the guts to go out and put ourselves out on the line to that same extent, the least you can do is make a noise about it and try to support them. These are very wonderful people facing severe punishment.

BONPANE: I remember, back in 1968, that Phil Berrigan invited thirteen of us to meet at 1620 S Street in Washington, D.C. and he had spoken about the fact that they intended to remove the draft files from the Catonsville, Maryland Draft Board and bring those files into the parking lot and to napalm them to ask the question, "Is it better to burn paper or people?" That action created a stir nationally and was imitated over a hundred times in different ways. Some people seemed very shocked that they would burn paper, and then they did have the opportunity to say, "Well look what's happening in Vietnam." So nine of those people in the basement became part of that. In all of those actions throughout the United States, there were no injuries, there was no violence to people. It was a powerful statement of a mutation that seemed to be taking place in the thinking of the people of the United States. So I think these are important acts that are generally not covered very heavily by the media, but they'll be known nevertheless.

SCHELL: Yes, they will be and they are. One of the things I most respect about these people is their willingness to continue in the absence of media attention and so forth. That's really when it's the hardest, being the "winter soldier" of protest. Its far easier to be one in a crowd of millions than to be out there all by yourself facing prison sentences with the nation's gaze turned somewhere else.

BONPANE: This is why I consider them to be a vanguard. The three Dominican sisters in Northeastern Colorado just recently attacked a missile silo on the ground. Once again, they poured their blood on it and they hammered the earth around it and they are facing some thirty years in prison. They feel its that important to make the point that we could have a planet that looks like Mars or Pluto but just doesn't have anyone living on it. So I'm so happy that you focused in on the matter of nonviolence and the will of the people. I think once people understand what the voices of these gentle souls are saying, "Happy are the gentle; they shall possess the earth" it seems like the earth is going to be saved by the gentleness of the people who can make a strong statement without harming anyone, but say, "Look folks, you're on a road to suicide and we'd like you to turn around before its too late." So I think that's the position we're in at this time. In terms of a treaty, for instance the Charter of the United Nations, it becomes incarnate in the Constitution of the United States, and in violating the treaty we're violating the Constitution. How long can our governmental disobedience continue before we reach a place where we've gone too far?

SCHELL: Well, the United Nations is a collection of nations. It's not a country in its own right. People like to pound on the United Nations and criticize it for one thing or another. And I've criticized it myself. But that always seems to me to kind of miss the point because the United Nations is nothing other than the collected representatives of the nations of the earth. And of course, within its structure, the most important, or the most decisive voices are those given a veto—the five powers in the Security Council, including of course the United States. If one of those powers, and right now it's the United States, becomes obstructive and declines to work together with the others on the Council and in the United Nations, then it simply cannot work. And there's no point in pounding on something called the "United Nations." You have to look at the nations that are a part of it, and in this case I think it's the United States that is really standing most detrimentally in the way.

BONPANE: Well we've seen that consistently now with the opposition to the International Criminal Court, with the opposition to the various resolutions of the U.N., and I fully agree that it isn't a time to trash the U.N. for that reason, it's a time to identify the fact that the great singular superpower is not happy to work with the U.N. unless its doing exactly what we want. I was in Nicaragua when the World Court heard the case of Nicaragua vs. U.S. and the Court decided that we were supposed to pay $17 billion and we simply wouldn't do it. So

216

you kind of destroy the jurisdiction of a court if you refuse to comply with it. I'm very concerned with that in terms of the future. Now this concept of what is brought up here is the concept of "world federalism." I know you have a good deal in your book about the whole concept of federalism. Would you consider a functional U.N. as a world federalist body?

SCHELL: If the current U.N. were to work perfectly it still wouldn't be considered federalism because its structured in a way that gives each of the permanent five that are on the Security Council that veto power. And no structure that has, really, an unfettered veto power could honestly be called a federal one. So federalism is a much larger stretch than even a functional U.N. would be. For instance, if you look at the European Union, even there, they're having a debate about whether to call it a federal system or not. And there, they have a far greater degree of integration: monetary, economic, and now more and more social and political than the U.N. gets close to. So a federal system is still very far away.

BONPANE: I want our listeners to know that I'm speaking to Jonathan Schell, the author of many books, and the author of a brand new book that is extremely striking in its insight: *The Unconquerable World: Power, Nonviolence, and the Will of the People*. Its just out and I highly recommend this book because of its importance for our time. Jonathan, we have a book written by our former Attorney General called *The Fire This Time*, by Ramsey Clark. He speaks about the restructuring of the U.N., suggesting that the Security Council be abolished and that a true legislative branch be developed whereby every member of the legislative branch would represent the world by population and their work there would be to represent the world rather than their country. Have you seen his suggestions for restructuring?

SCHELL: No, I haven't read those, I'm sorry to say.

BONPANE: I think there's a lot worthy of consideration there. He feels that there should be an executive branch, that we can have a legislative branch if we make these changes and eliminate the victor's justice of the Security Council and that we could have a body that would sound like more of a world federalist body at this time because the problems you mentioned regarding federalism would no longer be there. I think he has a rather Jeffersonian approach to all of this and I also recommend that book, *The Fire This Time* by former Attorney General, Ramsey Clark.

SCHELL: Well I look forward to reading that.

217

BONPANE: Great. There's so much here and I think another very important issue that you go into is something that is usually not understood. It's the whole question of sovereignty. What that means: whether the sovereign is the king, the parliament, the congress, the people, the sovereignty of people as was at least suggested in the formation of our own country. Are we a sovereign people?

SCHELL: Well, just at the minute we're trying to be something rather more than sovereign; we're trying to be dominant over others, breaching the sovereignty of others. So it goes beyond, really, an assertion even of absolute sovereignty, with what the United States is doing now. The problem with sovereignty as I see it, at the root, and whether you're talking about a sovereignty of kings, or of legislature, or even of the people, is that it asserts an absolute power of one's own political system to make its decision without any reference whatsoever to the interests or decisions or options of others. And to me, this flies into the face of the reality of life in the world, which is one of international interdependence. So it introduces an anarchic note into a reality that has already gone far beyond a system of separate and independent nation-states, if any such thing ever did exist, and it never really did, but it exists less so now than ever before. So there's really a vast array of problems and opportunities ranging from the very mundane, such as international telephone and mail standards and so forth, all the way up to global warming that really in principle cannot be dealt with by any single nation.

BONPANE: You mention something striking here from Madison in the Federalist Papers where he states that the true distinction of the American Constitution lies in the total exclusion of the people in their collective capacity from any share of the government. It was a fact that the people using their powers to amend the Constitution, could both legally and peacefully pull down the whole edifice, including their own amending power, and in that sense were supreme, yet it was no less true in the ordinary business of government the people were barred from directly making almost any decision. Do I have some kind of contradictory thing here?

SCHELL: It's part of the subtlety and really the genius of the American system in my opinion. In a certain sense, the people are supreme. In other words, the people can vote to amend the constitution. The bill goes right out of existence. They can do absolutely anything they want in that sense. What the people cannot do in any given instance is pass legislation or to create a judicial decision. In order to have a

218

judicial decision that you want—lets say the people want to outlaw abortion—they have to elect three or four presidents in a row who would appoint five or six or seven Supreme Court justices in a row who would undo that. In other words, it's a sovereignty that in a certain sense, or a power that in a certain sense is unreserved but paid out in small pieces, so to speak. This does strike me as being quite wise because it avoids and heads off the problem that a temporary majority could in a single action pull down the whole edifice. It's as if to say that the people consist of more than one generation. It's as if to say that the people consist of more than the living. You'd have to have a couple of generations succeeding one another to carry out change that would be as drastic as that.

BONPANE: Well let's look at it again from the base. You're referring to the nonviolent movement. We see so many examples today. We see the great work of the School of the Americas watch. Fr. Roy Bourgeois pulls together over 10,000 people a year at Fort Benning, Georgia to demand the closure of the School of the Americas, and he himself has spent five years in prison out of a decade to make his point. This constant development from the base seems to be promoting exactly what you're talking about. It seems to be what you're talking about here is forming or building a peace system to replace an outdated war system.

SCHELL: Yes, well the people who carry out those protests again are people who are taking responsibility, really, in their own person and their own suffering for what their countries are doing. To me, one of the great new facts of the twentieth, and now the twenty-first century, is something that I think we don't notice enough and haven't pulled together, which has been the incredible power and political effectiveness of nonviolent change and nonviolent revolution. After all, Mohandas Gandhi had as much to do as any other single person with the downfall of the British Empire, which was the greatest of its time. And then if we look at the Soviet Empire, closer to us historically, we find that once again in the Solidarity movement in Poland or in the movement in Czechoslovakia, that they mounted a kind of resistance within a totalitarian system that was a specific political process that unraveled all of that and they did that—I'd like to quote Lech Walesa who said to the joint session of Congress, "We did it without breaking a single pane of glass."

BONPANE: I think that the trick here is the effectiveness of nonviolence.

SCHELL: Well it is. It's a tremendous—its not an abstraction, its not only an ideal now. We have at least a century of experience with it and immense historical epic-making changes that have been brought about

219

by it. So we have to look at it not only as an idea, but as an immense historical reality that has created new foundations that we can build on. Foundations, by the way, did not exist in 1919 or 1945 when the League of Nations and the United Nations were created.

BONPANE: Well we have now, even the AFL-CIO, this summer planning a Freedom Ride based on the Freedom Rides of 1961. They're going to have immigrants depart from cities all over the United States with a Freedom Ride to Washington to call attention to the needs of a living wage and the needs of the social rights of people who have come here from other lands. So we're seeing this is contagious. You mentioned that fear is contagious, and it certainly is—sickeningly so—but that courage is also contagious. So it seems that one after another, we're seeing such examples of massive nonviolent statements, none of which is greater than the International Human Rights march, which is going to take place in Palestine and Israel, partially under the direction of Torrill Eide. Torrill was part and parcel of our march through Central America in '85-'86. She's back. She's gone to the Israeli government to get clearance, spoken to the Palestinians. She understands diplomacy—which I wish many of our lawmakers would understand—and in a very diplomatic manner is going to say, "Look, we are not a partisan march. We are marching on behalf of peace and international rights." And so far, she's had a lot of encouragement.

SCHELL: Sounds like those are good things to hear about and to participate in.

BONPANE: Indeed, I have been very touched by the fact that they're going ahead. This will start September 4th and will go through September 25 of this year. Our listeners should know I'm talking to Jonathan Schell. He's the author of many works, including *The Fate of the Earth* and now *The Unconquerable World Power: Nonviolence and the Will of the People*. Jonathan, we have a terrible time sometime with the will of the people because of the enormous power of media and enormous power of sound bites that are sometimes rather silly, and actually also the power of occasional, flat out lies. I had Scott Ritter with us here in Los Angeles over the weekend, and he was just saying, "Well, the government has been lying to us and the media has been complicit in those lies."

SCHELL: Well, he had it right from the start. I heard him speak a couple of times.

BONPANE: Yeah, he's amazing. I mean, here's an example of a person coming out of the Republican party, a long history in the Marine Corps, finally made the Chief Weapons Inspector for the United Nations, not the United States, but for the whole United Nations, and he made it very clear what was not taking place in Iraq and he's come against the power of the president, by virtue of lies, and he feels that this has led to the death of his buddies—his Marine Corps buddies—and to the death of many innocent people in Iraq as well. So he's truly outraged at what has taken place and I think its reached a state where our own structures are trying to discredit him at this time rather than to listen to his case.

SCHELL: Well, I think we've reached that point a while ago. They were trying to get rid of him. He really has a right to call us up short because he was saying that there was no proof of weapons of mass destruction many months before the war began—even a year as I recall. So he was one of the few who had that right, or the factual basis for making such a claim.

BONPANE: You mention in your book, in *The Logic of Peace*, the chief instrument being direct action, which is both non-cooperative and constructive, but is also the wellspring of the people's will in democratic nations. It is therefore mighty on the defensive, feeble on the offensive. I wonder what you mean by that.

SCHELL: Well, what I mean is that I think that there is a principle and a very good one. That is people should be in charge of their own affairs, of their own domestic affairs. This is sort of the positive aspect of sovereignty or the principle of which sovereignty is sort of a perversion, if you will. And so, to me it makes great sense that people should manage their own affairs and what that means is that their power is strong at home. So their power is strong where they live because they are living as they wish and don't wish to be disrupted by other countries. But, if they try, as the military folks say, to project their power half-way across the world the way the United States is trying to do in Iraq today, then it becomes perverted. Then it becomes unjust and wrong because, naturally, those people there want to manage their own affairs. So that is why I say a genuine power of the people that is rooted on the home soil is very mighty there, but that it is very weak elsewhere in the world. And by the way, that is not withstanding the tremendous military machine and superiority that the United States has. I think we're running into a buzz saw now of popular resistance within Iraq. You know, I'm not romantic about that country. I don't know what system they might put up. They might make a terrible mistake and put up another dictatorship. What I am quite sure of though is that it is not within our power to bring them whatever politics they're going to wind up with. I think we're going to just bloody ourselves and them and a lot of other people by trying to do that.

BONPANE: Well, the President seems to imply that the war was over when he spoke on the aircraft carrier and we're losing troops every day and according to Scott Ritter, there are about forty Iraqis dying every day, so that it appears the war is not over and I just can't believe the impossibility of those in power to learn from history. I mean we could have learned something from the war in Indochina, which we lost absolutely, totally, after having all of that firepower—and here we go repeating the same errors and even seeming surprised at the people.

SCHELL: Yes, well we seem almost—some of this is terribly simple. In other words, I think people in other countries are much more like Americans than we tend to think. All you have to do is imagine the reaction of some other country. Let's say France were to come over here and start telling us how to pick up our garbage or to run the City Hall or what programs we could put on television or what economic system we could have or what cheese we could eat or what have you—you know, we wouldn't stand for that for a quarter of a second and it turns out that other people around the world feel the same way and they're really willing to make that stick and to sacrifice for that.

BONPANE: Well, what happened in 1917 when the British took over in Iraq and told the people that ages of oppression have now ended? The people in Iraq didn't seem to agree with them.

SCHELL: They certainly didn't, and of course they threw the British out as all of the colonial people did. But by now that verdict is in. Empire has been a universal failure. It has been rejected by the world. So for the United States to get back into the imperial business, and in effect try to reinvent it for the 21st century, its not only wrong but a colossal error and it's something that we shouldn't wish to see work, but also something that can't work.

BONPANE: Well, its so disturbing to see the lack of leadership. The king of England praised the first President of the United States for not wanting to be in power for life and said that it appears you're going to have a great future as a result of that. Leaders must have an understanding of the importance of change. We should lead in peacemaking by supporting the elimination of the weapons of mass destruction from the face of the earth through cooperative work. The word "cooperative" is very frequent in your book. But I think I hear "compete" about 50 times a day, and I think if we learn "cooperate" and what it really means, it would have a great impact on the legal system as well as on the whole political system.

SCHELL: Well, I mean, the law is of course nothing but a formalized system of cooperation. So the very essence of the thing is that.

BONPANE: Well it's high time for us to understand. We have not shown leadership in the matter of nuclear weapons. In fact we're planning to build new ones. We're in great danger from our own weapons of mass destruction and looking for newer models just as we would be looking for a new model of an SUV or something and I think this is extremely dangerous. These weapons have a great possibility of accident and I think the more we threaten people with them, especially about preemptive use, we are creating a terrible environment throughout the world. Are you in touch with this expansion of the nuclear problem?

SCHELL: Very much so and nothing is more dangerous than that. I've spent more than the better part of a quarter of a century trying to think about it and write about it and once again, here as with the issue of self-determination, somehow the United States almost seems to have exempted itself from the human condition. We almost seem to be saying that across the board, whether that's economically, militarily or politically, we reserve the right to all kinds of privileges that we will go to war to eradicate in other countries and this double-standard is no more clearer than in the nuclear quest where not only do we sit on top of weapons of massive destruction, lecturing to others how terrible they are, but we even propose to use the ones we have to stop others from getting them. That's the sort of new wrinkle of policy there. And we're even inventing new nuclear weapons to cross the nuclear threshold again.

BONPANE: Think about how that empowers other people to say, "Well, maybe we can use them too." I mean, India and Pakistan, China and Taiwan, Russia and Chechnya—

SCHELL: Well, once again people around the world are more like us than we think. If we assert the right and other nuclear powers do, then other countries will want that too. They'll say, "Well, we don't want to be a second-class citizen in this world." It's human nature.

BONPANE: Well, Jonathan, one of the many ways of proving the similarities of people throughout the world is the agreement of the Universal Declaration of Human Rights. We have often heard critics say, "Well, your human rights aren't our human rights," but we have come to an agreement in this document that we do agree on human rights and that document is there and has been there for half a century. Is that some-

223

thing we can afford to ignore, that such a document actually exists?

SCHELL: You know, that document, and you can give other examples too, sometimes there will be a declaration that will not seem to take effect right away, and certainly that one didn't. And certainly today, its more the exception than the rule that its observed. Nevertheless what it does, and what it has done in many cases, is to provide a sort of rallying point for people to take incremental actions to very slowly and very gradually make it real. I think it is closer to reality now than it was in 1945, although reverses are always possible, and vigilance is the price of liberty and so forth. In general, I want to comment in regard again to the League of Nations and United Nations, which embody this essential dream of a world without war. This is a sensible dream, but what they did for all kinds of very excellent historical reasons is to do that from the governmental level rather than from the top. And if I think there is something new in our situation, its that whether we're talking about February 15 movement against the war or whether we're talking about the protest activity that you mentioned in this program, or whether we're talking about the universal rebellion against the empire, which has been utterly successful in the 21st century; what we have now is a potential to sort of create the foundation of peace on the ground as a real thing in real places. The betterment of human rights would be one example. Efforts even to improve the environment, even where people work cooperatively as I say, the end of empires, the nonviolent movements that have been so important, have created new tracks on the ground, as the military people like to say that are a new and different foundation on which we could build some things that are more successful than what we have tried to build in the past, even if we see it as rather slowly and incrementally.

BONPANE: Indeed, and what I'm concerned about is that our culture of militarism is having a profound effect on the domestic scene. One example of it is the prison system where we have 25% of the world's prisoners and only 5% of the world's people. I think this is an extension of domestic militarism.

SCHELL: It's like our pollution.

BONPANE: Indeed.

SCHELL: Pollution and prisoners seem to be the chief product.

BONPANE: Well, you should see Los Angeles today. I mean the air is a toxic sewer. Its visible everywhere you go, around this megapolis even on this very day, its really quite striking. I think if I were to injure one person's lungs I would be guilty of a felony, but for the corporate toxicity that damages millions of people's lungs, it apparently has no responsibility. So these are problems that relate to an aggressive military system. I hope we can turn it around. I think with books like yours, if you get people thinking about these things, we'll be able to make a step forward. What about your Gandhi and the use of the word "satyagraha?" Is that going to be with us for some time?

SCHELL: Oh yeah. I think that he was the Thomas Edison or the Einstein or the Galileo of nonviolence. He had an insight that I think was very fundamental for his period and ours, which is that political power and governmental power even depends, not only should it depend on the people it governs, but it actually does so. It actually does depend on the consent of the government and the support of the government and on the support of the governed. And if people withdraw their support from a government, then their power is at an end. And I think that is what we did see with the British power, and even with the Soviet one, by the way. And that's an enduring lesson that has been taught to us in the 20th century and it happens that Gandhi has been the pioneer of it.

BONPANE: I think that the single myth in our culture in our time is the myth of powerlessness. We are enormously powerful. We have tremendous power and act in concert especially with non-cooperation. We don't cooperate with things that we feel are immoral or illegal, and once we become aware of the power we have, I think we'll move forward and we're seeing that each day. I mean in this city and in the United States and throughout the world, so I have great hopes for the non-cooperation. I think its important for the people to understand the theory that people in government are to behave as servants. We use that word and they should realize that they are to act like servants and behave like servants and that the people are empowered to insist that their will be known. And sometimes, we hear our people respond as though they lived in a monarchy, which we hope we don't.

SCHELL: Yes, in fact, I think that the power that's available to people is actually unlimited. But as you say, if you think of power in another way, it seems the other way around. But once you understand what I think the great pioneers of nonviolence understand, is that without the consent or supportive activity of the governed for the government there is no state.

BONPANE: You state here in one of your final statements whether combined with violence, as in the people's war, sustained by a constitution as in democracy, or standing alone such as Satyagraha, or living in truth, it is becoming the final arbiter of the public affairs of our time and the political bedrock of our unconquerable world. In other words, the time has come for this type of power to be unveiled, you might say.

SCHELL: I think it is that time, and I think it sort of is half-unveiled already and what has to be done now is to pull away the veil altogether.

BONPANE: Well, its extremely important for all of us to realize that we work from the base in our work and are privileged daily with some of the people I have mentioned in this program, including the Voices in the Wilderness that I personally met in Iraq in 1991. There was Cathy Kelly at that time, and people who were called the "Iraq Peace Team." And I simply couldn't believe what they were doing. I mean they went down to the Saudi border and they camped there right with the threat of war moving over them, saying, "We've got to make this statement." And they've continued. They were there all through the embargo, they were there through the recent conflict, and they are still very active today. And I think they are more in touch with reality than many of the very highest powers in politics are. And this is the curious thing. These are people who are world-class in their simplicity and their depth at the same time. Have you heard of their work?

SCHELL: Oh yeah, absolutely. Remarkable.

BONPANE: I find it to be that way. I think its this type of behavior that will hopefully be the mark of the 21st century while we're dealing with governmental policy that is almost classically 19th century. It's a little disturbing at times but I have high hopes that we can rise to the occasion and be able to overcome all of this. I want all of our listeners to know that today I have been speaking with Jonathan Schell who is the author of so many works. *The Time of Illusion*, *The Fate of the Earth*, and *The Village of Ben Suc*. He has been a contributor to *The Nation, Harpers, The Atlantic*, and *Foreign Affairs*. He has taught at Wesley and Princeton University and Emory, among other universities. He is currently Harold Willens Peace Fellow at The Nation Institute. Any final advice for us at this time Jonathan as a prologue to your book or afterward?

SCHELL: I feel as many people feel about the direction our country is going in, and when you see the forces that are arrayed against us, its pretty daunting. Someone said that all four branches of government are under control of one party. But actually, I think that underneath all of that there is a new foundation and if we could get back onto a better path, we would find that there is solid ground underfoot. And that's something that we couldn't have said maybe 25, 50, or 75 years ago. So there is a reason for hope as far as I'm concerned.

BONPANE: Well I fully agree and I think we're seeing more and more of the gentle people of the earth on the way to possessing the land and having a greater future and just want to thank you so much for being with us today, Jonathan Schell. Your works have been a great contribution to the people of the world and I know we'll be hearing a great deal about your book, *The Unconquerable World*.

Chalmers Johnson

II

August 15, 2003

BONPANE: Hello, and welcome to *World Focus*. I'm Blase Bonpane. We're very privileged today to have Dr. Chalmers Johnson with us. Professor Johnson has served on the faculties of the University of California at Berkeley as well as the University of California San Diego. Dr. Johnson is President of the Japan Policy Research Institute and has written many books, including *Blowback: The Costs and Consequences of American Empire*. Now we must ready ourselves for his forthcoming book, *The Sorrows of Empire: Militarism, Secrecy, and the End of the Republic*. Forthcoming from Metropolitan Books and in London from Verso Books. Welcome, Dr. Chalmers Johnson.

JOHNSON: Thank you, it's always a privilege to be here.

BONPANE: Well, it's wonderful to have you on. As a result of those sorrows, you state that, "their cumulative effect guarantees that the United States will cease to resemble the country outlined in the Constitution of 1787." You mention that "there will be a state of perpetual war leading to more terrorism against Americans wherever they may be, and a spreading reliance on nuclear weapons among smaller nations as they try to ward off the imperial juggernaut." That is Sorrow number one. Would you care to comment?

JOHNSON: In part, the subtitle of my new book, "The End of the Republic," is a reference to the end of the Roman republic because it reminds me of this particular time. In the '40s BC, Rome was a genuine republic with one of the most complex sets of checks and balances ever invented and had lasted for nearly 250 years. But it had now begun to acquire an empire and found its political institutions were not up to dealing with that. Indeed, a state of perpetual war leading ultimately to civil war had begun to overwhelm the place. Of course Caesar came to power in an attempt to end this by creating an autocracy that turned into a tyranny leading to his own death at the hands of conservatives. But then they were unable to govern, and further civil war developed

228

until finally the Roman republic simply gave up and turned itself over to Caesar's god-nephew, Octavian, who of course then became a self-proclaimed god and Augustus Caesar, the first emperor. And the rest, as they say, is history: a military dictatorship.

BONPANE: The parallel is amazing and we could look at other empires as well, even the indigenous empires of the Mayans and the Aztecs, to say nothing of the Spaniards and the British. And here we go again. So the first step that you have identified is this perpetual war phenomenon.

JOHNSON: What I mean is that once you have an empire, then many consequences follow from that. You need an army to police it. In the case of the Roman republic, traditionally armies were simply raised from farmers off the land who then returned to the land when the war was over. As the Roman empire developed, in the time of Marius, they began to develop standing armies. This then created those famous problems when the armies were disbanded. Now the soldiers wanted land to be given to them, and this began to conflict with the old power structure of Rome, one thing leading to another. One reason I find the Roman comparison so apt today is because there seem to be enthusiasts for Rome in Washington who know almost nothing about it, and another is the fact that one of the most cherished rights of Romans was, of course, not slaves but their faith in free speech. At the time of Caesar's dictatorship, you have Cicero beginning to talk about how people guard their voices . . . they must be careful now. Caesar was a tyrant, but he also seems to have been smarter and more forward thinking than many of the conservatives in Washington who have allowed our sorry state to come to pass.

BONPANE: Well, Dr. Johnson, in the midst of all of this, you have the phenomenon of militarism, which I think is one of the most important issues that can be studied in the history of war. And it's so often neglected.

JOHNSON: That's what I actually try to deal with in my new book: *Militarism and Its Effects on Our Society*. I can fairly easily imagine how, with the scandals overcoming this administration, if there is some decent alternative candidate, George Bush could be defeated at the polls. What I can't quite imagine is the defeat of the Pentagon. Regardless of who wins the 2004 election, we run into the military industrial complex, the growing militarism in our society, the influence—as at the end of the Roman republic—of former soldiers. So, indeed, I think perpetual war is a way of saying that every empire, once it gets launched, starts discovering that it's got to wage still further wars to

229

protect what it has, and this leads to an enlargement of the empire, but ultimately, inevitably, to overstretch and bankruptcy. But above all, a tremendous domestic repercussion of the movement towards trying to defend this empire simply leads to tyranny.

BONPANE: We seem to have an absence here of what is called diplomacy, and we are, the world is, hungry for diplomacy while we're involved in a mean-spirited dictatorial policy of just speaking in terms of ultimata, rather than speaking in humane terms. And this has had an impact on the domestic situation where we have become number one in the imprisonment of people.

JOHNSON: I agree with you, and one of the most foreboding signs is the degree to which diplomacy is now in the hands of the military.

BONPANE: They're not trained for this.

JOHNSON: Exactly. The American regional commanders report directly to the President and the rest of the world sees primarily heavily armed, uniformed Americans as representatives of the country—not representatives of AID, or the State Department, or even American businesses compared to the intrusiveness of our military. So, indeed, we do not seem to have a foreign policy any more: we just have an empire.

BONPANE: One problem you try to identify is the difficulty of acknowledging the number of casualties among people who served, for example, in Iraq War I. You came up with a figure of 30 percent casualties among our forces. Now I don't think that people understand the reality that about 30 percent of those troops are now on disability.

JOHNSON: Yes, a great many of them have died or been disabled from the effects of depleted uranium. This ammunition used by our armed forces, even more extensively in Gulf War II. It is armor penetrating, but it releases uranium 238, which has deadly consequences. Every time I saw a picture of the sandstorms during the battles moving north toward Baghdad or I see children playing on a burnt-out tank or climbing into a building that has been hit with a cruise missile, I feel like saying, "You should be wearing some kind of protective device in order not to inhale stuff that's in the air." It has had unbelievable consequences from the First Gulf War. We have had almost a third of General Schwarzkopf's army applying for disability benefits from the Veterans' Administration.

BONPANE: Let's look at the exact data that you give us. You state, "In May of 2002, the Veterans Administration reported that an additional 8,306 soldiers had died and 159,705 were injured or ill as a result of service-connected exposures suffered during the war. Even more alarmingly, the Veterans Administration revealed 206,861 veterans—almost a third of General Schwartzkopf's entire army, had filed claims for medical care, compensation and pension benefits based on injuries and illnesses caused by combat in 1991." Now is this going to be worse in this current war?

JOHNSON: Well, I think there's no doubt that the human consequences will be tragic. I was recently speaking to some Marines here in San Diego who were just back from Iraq and they asked for my advice. And I had to say, "Don't have children," because among the consquences of depleted uranium we're beginning to see very serious birth deformities in the children of those who've been exposed to it. But also, what one ought to stress here is that this becomes extremely expensive, not just in terms of deaths. Those who have survived but are crippled become a very large pressure group after a while with quite legitimate claims against the government, which is already in a severe financial crisis.

BONPANE: Well, we had a report from the Pentagon that they couldn't account for a trillion dollars, that's with a "t," and that there will be no audit to find out what happened to that "pocket change." This is unheard of.

JOHNSON: It's actually a greater amount than that paid annually in income tax. The Constitution itself contains really powerful clauses on the need for the public in an informed democracy to know how its money is spent. But you can't make an informed decision about how your money is being spent because, like the Manhattan Project during World War II, all of the intelligence budget and 40 percent of the Defense budget is secret—secret not only to the public but even to the overwhelming majority of the people's representatives.

BONPANE: When we pay our income tax we're allowed to determine where $3 goes, aren't we? That is really quite impressive. This phenomenon leads to what you call "the Second Sorrow" or "loss of democracy and Constitutional rights." As the presidency eclipses congress, it is transformed from a co-equal executive branch of government into a military junta. This is really a worrisome thing. It is one of the things that worried George Washington when he warned against the influence of a large standing army in his Farewell Address.

JOHNSON: Yes, the two most famous generals who were President—that is, George Washington and Dwight Eisenhower—warned us in their farewell addresses of the enormous dangers of that most characteristic institution of militarism, the standing army. We even disbanded the military after World War II. Of course, very soon with the onset of the

231

Cold War, we were back at it. But, the thing that's alarming is that with the end of the Cold War, we made no effort at all to return to a Constitutional foreign policy.

BONPANE: We came into a perpetual war economy at that time. Now what concerns me very much, Dr. Johnson, is the numbness of all of us. Where is the sense of outrage or how has that been channeled into something else?

JOHNSON: I don't know the answer. That's one of the reasons I'm writing a sequel to *Blowback*. *Blowback* was actually written 18 months before 9/11, as a warning that the consequences of our foreign policy during the Cold War would result in retaliatory action against us and that the American public was unprepared for it because the actions that were leading to blowback had been largely kept secret from them. Now I think its no longer a time for a warning. As it stands right now, Articles 4 and 6 of the Bill of Rights are defunct: that is, *habeas corpus* and the right to privacy in your home. These have been suspended by the Patriot Act and by individual acts of the Department of Justice, the FBI, et cetera. We are moving into extremely dangerous waters these days. It's hard to believe that the Supreme Court will protect us, given that this is the Supreme Court that intervened in politics to give us this government.

BONPANE: Perhaps your "third Sorrow" is one of the answers for this numbness, this "psychic numbing." That is, "the replacement of truth by propaganda, disinformation and the glorification of war, power, and the military legions." Is that a reason for the numbness?

JOHNSON: Well, certainly it's part of it. We were told, as was the British public, that as a matter of our very safety, our national preservation, we had to attack Iraq in the most powerful, possible way—a country that had been under extreme sanctions for over a decade and had been defeated once before. We now know that we were lied to. Iraq was not a threat. The thing that was remarkable about Saddam Hussein was that he did not have weapons of mass destruction. What the North Koreans seem to have learned from the Iraq War is that you had better actually have them because it's the only thing that will cause the Americans to hold back.

BONPANE: That's the irony here.

JOHNSON: It is. And it is also the greatest incentive toward proliferation. Even Brazil at one time had a nuclear weapons program that it abandoned. But I must say, if I were Lula da Silva today, I would seriously talk with my advisors about what to do if the Americans decided to push us around.

BONPANE: Well, this is how it all began. I think that after Hiroshima and Nagasaki, the Soviet Union was asking the same question, saying that here's a country that uses these weapons against two civilian populations. We had better do something and do it fast. And now we're getting the whole world into that posture, creating a much larger cold, and possibly hot war.

JOHNSON: In the name of war on terror, we have made the world a much more dangerous place. We have virtually destroyed the system of international rules of which we had been the leading sponsor and developed over the postwar period. But now, for example, it's become simply impossible for anyone today to believe our Secretary of State.

BONPANE: Yes, this has become a major problem and perhaps is another one of the contributions to the sorrows. Investigative journalists are up to about their fortieth lie from the administration. We had former Ambassador Wilson here and had a chance to talk to him about this. He certainly brought out the issue of Niger and the lies connected with that.

JOHNSON: Yes, and it was an utterly illegal act for the government to reveal that his wife worked for the Central Intelligence Agency.

BONPANE: It's very, very dangerous and not legal to give the names of agents. And Wilson felt that this was a terrible slap at himself. He served under President Clinton and he apparently was the last man to speak to Saddam Hussein before the first war, and he was quite conversant about what was going on there.

JOHNSON: What he discovered in Niger was of course that the British had faked this intelligence. And now, in this morning's British press, it is revealed that Prime Minister Blair was deeply involved in an attempt to humiliate the scientist David Kelly, who committed suicide. These are monstrous scandals and to find something equivalent, I would suggest that one reread Shakespeare's *Julius Caesar*.

BONPANE: Now the "last Sorrow" that you list is "bankruptcy as the United States pours its economic resources into evermore grandiose military projects and shortchanges the education, health, and safety of its citizens." For example, we don't have much dental care in this country. About 70 percent of our children need dental care and they're not going to get it. If they lived in France they would receive that, but they live in this very poor country known as the United States where there is no dental care.

JOHNSON: Yes, the first three sorrows—warfare, loss of our constitutional

233

rights, and deceit in the government's speaking to the public—will ultimately lead to a crisis. But there's no question that bankruptcy leads to a crisis. We now have the largest national debt in our history. We are the world's leading debtor nation. This is not good even in comparison with other empires. Britain, on the eve of the First World War, had trade surpluses that were running at seven percent of gross national product. Britain was a very rich country and could afford a mistake such as the Boer War. The United States is running trade deficits, the greatest trade deficits ever recorded in history, that amount to five percent of our gross national product. And we're running out of the ability to pay for them in that we don't manufacture things in this country any more that we sell to other people. We're mostly specialists in finance capital, and it's not rocket science to predict that this is an unstable situation.

BONPANE: Dr. Johnson, do you have any idea of where the Congress of the United States is on this? I mean, they are supposed to control the purse. Are they awake?

JOHNSON: I think this is where the Roman comparison comes in. If one looks back to what happened to the Roman republic, one can clearly see that a government with elaborate checks and balances became inappropriate to the empire they were trying to maintain. In some ways I have a feeling this is what is happening to our Congress. Most of the people in Congress are, in fact, deeply engaged in fundraising activities that amount to structural corruption. But at the same time, it's not merely an individual ethical problem. Congress can't possibly do oversight of the Pentagon because the information simply isn't available to them.

BONPANE: We have a situation now where it appears that we have begun a classic occupation of a foreign country. It seems to me that Iraq has become our Palestine and shows all the same characteristics. These are not the cheering crowds that we had expected. We're losing our troops every day and Iraqis are losing their lives every day.

JOHNSON: To go back to the Roman comparison, the people of Rome became so desperate to manage what they had taken on that they simply gave up and decided they would take a general as their leader, namely Octavian, whom they then turned into the first Roman emperor. What this suggests to me is that we are probably waiting, not for a George Bush type character, but instead for a Juan Peron type, a populist militarist. That is what the past tells us is likely to come our way.

BONPANE: What concerns me, Dr. Johnson, is the religiosity of this whole

234

situation and its comparison to Rome. You said that Bush seems to compare himself to Jesus in his repeated statements, notably on September 20th, 2001 when he said, "Those who are not with us are against us," which duplicates Matthew 12:30.

JOHNSON: There are many of people in America who know where that line came from.

BONPANE: Indeed. "He who is not with me is against me." Well, the newspaper *Ha'aretz* in Israel quoted Bush as saying, "God told me to strike at Al Queda and I struck them. And he instructed me to strike Saddam, which I did." So much for imitation Bible-speak, but there it is.

JOHNSON: It's unbelievable, isn't it?

BONPANE: Yes, it's the religiosity that's quite frightening.

JOHNSON: But it's also an invocation of imperial authority—namely that it's beyond reason, beyond rational policy. And it is utterly corrosive of anything that might be called a community of citizens. The essence of democracy is that public opinion matters, that we have ways of removing an unsatisfactory politician, that we have an elaborate set of checks and balances, and a division of powers in the government. These are, I think, the defining attributes of a genuine democracy. Increasingly, however, our Congress is powerless. The movement toward an imperial presidency is simply overwhelming, as we see in the Congressional vote of October 2002, giving the President almost limitless power to go to war, including the use of nuclear weapons if he so chose.

BONPANE: Could you attempt to unravel the situation that is taking place in Korea where the nation, just as Germany, appears to want to reunite and we are rattling sabers.

JOHNSON: Again, I think it reflects our enormous vested interest in finding military solutions to problems. The American military has been in Korea since 1945, and of course since the end of the Korean War, in 1953, it has produced a total stalemate and the separation of a once unified country into two separate enclaves that have gone in different directions. North Korea is a failed communist regime. The end of the Cold War was a disaster for it. The two countries that kept it alive economically, Russia and China, today have extremely friendly and lucrative relations with South Korea. South Korea's leading trading partner today is China, not the United States. In the year 2000, the President of South Korea, Kim Dae-jung, took it as his own initiative to go north and see if there was some basis for reconciliation, for ending this last divided territory of the Cold War, and he met with the northern dictator, Kim Jong Il. This initiated a breakthrough. The North Koreans are attempting slowly, very tentatively, to come in from the cold and to duplicate much of what China has done over the last 20 or 30 years and to do it in such a way that its society is not totally destabilized. The North Korean leaders are very aware of the political consequences of being on the losing side during the Cold War and what it led to elsewhere. The East German leaders were put on trial in a unified Germany; the leaders of Romania were put up against a wall and shot; the Soviet Union descended into mafia capitalism. The North Koreans have good reasons not to move too hastily. But the fundamental problem for them, it seems to me, came in the President's State of the Union message in 2002 when he listed three nations—Iran, Iraq and North Korea—in his so-called "axis of evil," indicating that they were appropriate targets for our new doctrine of preventive war.

BONPANE: This at a time when the South Koreans and North Koreans were putting together a railroad to connect the two parts of their country.

JOHNSON: Kim Dae-jung, the President of South Korea, won the Nobel Peace Prize in the year 2000 for his efforts. We undercut our ally. Our Second Infantry division has been placed up near the demilitarized zone as a so-called trip wire. That is, in case of a North Korean invasion, it would guarantee war with the United States because it would guarantee American casualties during the first days of the war. Now the Secretary of Defense, Mr. Rumsfeld, is moving the Second Division south of the Han River and south of the capital, which strongly suggests not that we fear an attack from the North but that, in fact, we are preparing our own attack and do not wish to have our troops in the way. In the North, in Pyongyang, after the "axis of evil" speech, they saw Iraq being singled out for attack, and then, after a tremendous troop build up, being attacked and Baghdad being sacked as it had been in the 13th century by the Mongols. Under these circumstances, North Korea had to conclude, "We're on their list. They're coming after us next."

BONPANE: Well, wasn't China involved in the war in Korea in 1950? China was a big part of it. Now I can't help but wonder where is China today in regard to our saber rattling toward North Korea? Are they in any way trying to communicate with us on this matter?

JOHNSON: There's no question that China has more influence over what goes on in the Korean peninsula than anyone. We vastly overstate our influence. China's position, as it has been for the last 2000 years, is that they like a structurally divided Korea. Therefore, they're perfectly satisfied with a North Korea and a South Korea. They just don't want North Korea to collapse. They certainly do not want war on the Korean peninsula. The Chinese have been instrumental in trying to ease this situation, but China is, after all, a nuclear power. What they're up against, in this case, is the North Koreans saying, "It looks like the Americans plan to take us out." And almost like Churchill in the Battle of Britain, they're saying, "If we've got to go, let's take one with us." And what the North Koreans would like to take with them if they're attacked is the city of Seoul with its 11 million people, and as many American bases in Okinawa and Japanese cities as they could hit.

BONPANE: We were really worried about the possibility of nuclear war in the first Korean War and there was a great deal of discussion about that.

JOHNSON: Yes, MacArthur wanted to use nuclear weapons against China.

BONPANE: Indeed. And now we are looking for what are called "more usable" nuclear weapons.

JOHNSON: Yes. Unimaginable.

BONPANE: This is a very frightening term, because if they are more usable, they are more likely to be used.

JOHNSON: Both Korea and Taiwan today are situations that, if American militarists would leave them alone, will solve themselves. In South Korea, an extremely rich country at least 25 to 30 times richer than the North and twice as populous, the people have become quite confident that they know what to do. They have very friendly relations with China and are one of China's leading trading partners. They no longer fear North Korea. They actually believe there is a great deal of logic to the North Korean position. They've also come to distrust the United States since the economic crisis of 1997, which the American government virtually acknowledged that it caused in order to deal with potential competitors in East Asia, including the Republic of Korea. So there is very considerable anti-Americanism in South Korea right now.

BONPANE: It also appears to me that we have a question here with Japan.

JOHNSON: Yes, the Japanese are in a very peculiar situation. They are our leading satellite. They seem to like that relationship, or at least the government seems to like it. I think, it's actually disastrous for them. I think they should be like the rest of Asia, adjusting to the emergence of a rich, developing, and peace-loving China rather than becoming as hostile and belligerent as they are about it and North Korea. They've passed new laws in Japan to send Japanese troops to Iraq. Of all things, they're talking about their own need, as they put it, for a nuclear deterrent. The trend of events in Japan is not healthy. This is not to say that it is popular. The overwhelming mass of the population remains deeply pacifist. But the situation also reveals the weakness of the democracy that we imparted after World War II, as contrasted with the very powerful and strong democracy that exists in South Korea today. The situation on the Korean peninsula is extremely dangerous right now, but once again, we could solve it, possibly very magnificently, if we took the 37,000 members of the Second Infantry division and the Air Force at Osan Air Base and brought them all back to the United States. They're no longer needed. President Kim Dae-jung, after his visit in 2000 came back and wrote in the *Los Angeles Times*, "There will be no war in Korea now." If it were not for the presence of the American military, that probably would be true.

BONPANE: The people in the South are so tired of our presence. There's been one anti-American demonstration after another.

JOHNSON: There are over 100 American military bases located in South Korea. There are almost daily incidents of sexual violence, accidents, noise, environmental pollution, bar brawls, things of this sort, that are an insult to Korean sovereignty and to their self respect. I am a veteran of the Korean War and I remember being in Kunsan on the west coast after it had twice been in American hands and twice in Chinese hands. It was simply unimaginable, as I think back to that time, that this country could have produced a cute little car called the Hyundai Sonata driving around Southern California.

BONPANE: We also have the ongoing U.S. bombing practice in South Korea, similar to Vieques, and then we have this massive presence in Okinawa.

JOHNSON: Okinawa is just a seething volcano. The Americans refuse to acknowledge that they're living on the side of Vesuvius. When one of these places does finally explode, it will be the equivalent for us of the breaching of the Berlin Wall in 1989 for the Soviet Union. It brought down their entire position in Eastern Europe. Either Okinawa or South Korea could explode over another incident combined with the unfairness of the so-called Status of Forces Agreement. Under these SOFAs, American troops who've committed crimes against civilians cannot be tried in domestic courts. What the Americans don't seem to realize is that this is quite reminiscent of the extraterritoriality that foreign imperialists imposed on China from the Opium War until 1943. If you committed a crime in China, you were turned over to your consul to be tried according to your law on the racist grounds that no white man should be subjected to the barbarian law of China.

BONPANE: Dr. Johnson, in a recent article you quoted Thomas Jefferson as stating, "When the government fears the people, there is liberty. When the people fear the government, there is tyranny." This is quite a concern to us now in the matter of what are called civil liberties. We have 664 individuals from 42 countries, including children, in a concentration camp in Guantanamo, Cuba and they're beyond the reach of the Constitution according to our President. They've been designated as illegal combatants, which is a concept unknown to international law.

JOHNSON: It is something made up by the President.

BONPANE: If anything, they should have at least the rights of prisoners of war, which they have not enjoyed, and now we hear talk of the preparation of execution areas for them.

JOHNSON: The President, as almost a Roman emperor, a Caligula, has now assumed the power to designate someone a "bad guy." Even native-born citizens, such as Padilla and Hamdi, have been denied their rights, above all to *habeas corpus* as stated in Article 4 of the Bill of Rights. These people are locked up in military prisons and the Attorney General, speaking in federal court, argues that federal judges have no right to question the military in wartime. But this is not wartime.

BONPANE: You mentioned in your book that Bush often speaks as if he were a modern Caligula, the Roman emperor who reigned from 37 to 41 AD, and who wanted to appoint his horse to the Senate. The appointments that Bush has made have been the equivalent. Each one seems to be the worst possible choice for each position. It is a rogues' gallery, including many convicted criminals. We have the largest number of convicts who have been put into government in the history of our country, and once again we're kind of stunned by the public acceptance of much of this.

JOHNSON: There is, as you were saying earlier, a tremendous problem of people being well informed. The press, obviously, is not helpful. Certainly, the television news is devoted to sensationalism. The few bright spots are on the Internet.

BONPANE: Yes, we're very proud of what's taking place on the Internet. These wonderful new magazines are reaching millions and millions of people. *Alternet, Move On, Antiwar.com* are doing a good job.

JOHNSON: But a poll says that maybe only 30 percent of the population—and indeed this 30 percent includes you and I—gets their news from the Internet or the *Nation* magazine, and I'm sorry to say that's about it. Still, 30 percent of a country as big as this one is a very large number of people.

239

BONPANE: Indeed, so what's happening is a division among people in our country, which we certainly hope won't develop into another conflict, but this separation is notable at the present time.

JOHNSON: Let's talk for a moment about civil conflict in the United States. We now have for the first time a so-called Northern Command, a new military command to deal with domestic threats in North America. This has never existed before. It was not created during World War II, when Congress quite explicitly feared such a unit would be the focus for military intervention into politics. It was never allowed during the Civil War. The danger is that, in case of civil conflict, the military would arrogate to itself the right to "maintain stability." That would be the end of the republic. It might not make the United States a hopeless place to live, but it certainly would not be the place we have in mind when we think of the United States, or the way departments of political science in our universities teach American government.

BONPANE: The Central Intelligence Agency was also not supposed to engage in domestic matters, and this is a transition that is now taking place, bringing this international agency into domestic affairs.

JOHNSON: Yes, we also have special operations, that is covert operations, being run increasingly out of the Pentagon. This is one of the major issues before Congress right now because the military is not required to submit a so-called finding for the President's signature in order to carry out a clandestine mission. The military has been engaged in special operations in Iraq that strongly suggest it is out of control.

BONPANE: We're coming into an era of elections now, so we're looking for some alternatives. We've seen a few candidates on the Democratic side that show some life. In the past election, many of us voted for the Greens, leading to the ire of many Democrats. We do see many people like Dennis Kucinich speaking about Bush's failings. Do you think there is a possibility of a realignment taking place?

JOHNSON: Well, I think one of the things that did happen as a result of the 2000 election is that a lot of people now believe that party does matter, that protest votes of the sort for Ralph Nader are simply meaningless within the system. However, what is interesting, I think, is the battle for leadership of the Democratic Party. You have so many influential incumbent Democrats arguing that Howard Dean is unelectable, whereas it seems to me that the only life one sees today are people like Dean and Kucinich, who are out there saying Bush lied. The attempt to duplicate the President's position or to avoid issues like militarism is simply self-destructive.

240

BONPANE: I remember being in Sacramento a few years back and there was a little gentleman there who came out of nowhere and was introducing himself around. He said, "My name is Jimmy Carter. I'd like to be President." And I thought, "Gee, this guy doesn't have a chance." But he did it. Now perhaps your "final sorrow" is the thing that may change the political climate here. You say, "the final sorrow is financial ruin. It is different from the other three in that bankruptcy may not be as fatal to the American Constitution as endless war, loss of liberty and habitual lying, but it is the only sorrow that will certainly lead to a crisis," and I think that may help us out.

JOHNSON: Well, we see the crisis coming. It's certainly out there. If the people in East Asia who invest their savings decide their money is more safely invested in Euros than in dollars, that ends the United States right then and there. The stock exchange collapses, we have a howling recession, and interest rates go off the chart in order to finance our huge debts, because you now have to pay people big money to get them to loan you their money.

BONPANE: The Euro seems to be supplanting the dollar even in the oil industry in many cases. This is quite a phenomenon.

JOHNSON: Yes, it is astonishing that our war in Iraq, this meaningless war that was allegedly to protect us from terrorism, has had the result of uniting Europe once and for all. Professors of international relations always used to teach that a principle American foreign policy was that we never wanted to see any kind of an alliance between France, Germany, and Russia. Well, we now have France, Germany, and Russia united against our policies.

BONPANE: Well, perhaps we have to look at the positive side of the Bush administration. He has given us the largest international peace movement in the history of the world.

JOHNSON: It's simply unbelievable that every democratic nation, even including our own, has expressed its opposition to this war.

BONPANE: On February 15th, 2003, we had tens of millions of people on the same day at the same time in countries throughout the globe making that point.

JOHNSON: Very powerful.

BONPANE: Very definitely, and it wasn't simply against the Iraq War; it was really against war. They feel the time has come to put the goals and objectives of the Charter of the United Nations into practice.

JOHNSON: Well, this is one of the positive signs, I think. It began in Seattle in late 1999. But the way this movement has grown and spread, it's

241

much more powerful and much more diverse than the inchoate efforts against the Vietnam War that took so long to develop.

BONPANE: It seems that we're running out of time, Professor Johnson, so I want to thank you so much for being with us today.

JOHNSON: It's always a pleasure to be here, and let me compliment you on the many things you've stood for, particularly your crusade against the U.S. Army's School of the Americas.

BONPANE: Well thank you so much and I hope that all our listeners will read your book, *The Sorrows of Empire: Militarism, Secrecy, and the End of the Republic*.

Chalmers Johnson
III

January 11, 2004

BONPANE: Hello this is Blase Bonpane with "World Focus." I'm very honored today to have Dr. Chalmers Johnson as our guest. Dr. Johnson is president of the Japan Policy Research Institute, a nonprofit public affairs organization devoted to public education concerning Japan and international relations in the Pacific. He taught at the University of California at both Berkeley and San Diego for 30 years. He's an endowed chair of Asian politics in both universities. He served as chairman at the Center of Chinese Studies and chairman of the Department of Political Science. He wrote the wonderful book, *Blowback: The Costs and Consequences of American Empire*, which appeared well before 9/11 and was very prescient in its analysis of what was about to happen. And now we're going to see the release of another great book on January 13, next Tuesday, *The Sorrows of Empire: Militarism, Secrecy, and the End of the Republic*. Welcome, Dr. Johnson.

JOHNSON: Thank you very much. It's always an honor to be here.

BONPANE: Dr. Johnson, I'm very concerned about the inability of empires to learn. Why is there no learning process? Empires seem to repeat and repeat. Do you have any thoughts on that?

JOHNSON: Empire have as its nature hubris, arrogance, overreaching. It seems inconsistent that someone who would set out on an imperial project would be at the same time self-reflective and understanding to appreciate that they're overextending themselves, that nemesis awaits them. I'm generally thinking you're quite right. Very few empires that I can think of voluntarily dismantle themselves. About the only example I can think of is Mikhail Gorbachev and the dismantling of the Soviet Union in 1989, when Gorbachev was willing to give up the Soviet empire in Eastern Europe in return for the restoration of friendly and normal relations between Russia and Western Europe, which was actually Germany and France.

243

BONPANE: Dr. Johnson, one of the sorrows that I see is the military families that are speaking out about their losses. The fact that we have no pictures of returned caskets, we have no reference to the wounded. There's no count of the Iraqi dead. There's no measure of the mentally and morally violated troops. All of that, that's part of the sorrow I believe.

JOHNSON: Well, let me just say in the subtitle of my new book, *The Sorrows of Empire*, the subtitle is *Militarism, Secrecy, and the End of the Republic*. It's really focuses on something that's usually taboo to discuss in this country—militarism—even though we've had warnings from famous generals, including George Washington, and perhaps most famously in recent years by Dwight Eisenhower in his farewell address when he invented the phrase "military industrial complex." But you're quite right to say that one of the elements of militarism today is the fact that the armed forces are, of course, voluntary. They have been so since 1973. It is not an obligation of the citizenship to defend the country. This means that today our armed forces, despite the fact that our Pentagon would like you to think otherwise, the armed forces are not a citizen army. Those with experience in World War II, or in my case, Korea or in the Vietnam War, would probably not recognize the armed forces today. The old chores, including guard duty, KP, and cleaning latrines, these are usually farmed out to civilian companies that are given very lucrative contracts, including Dick Cheney's Halliburton Company. But of course, these are the dynamics within the armed forces. One of the things I try to go into in the new book is why people join the armed forces today. And to a very large extent, it's to escape from some dead end job in society or as a route of social mobility for people who find the future of their lives frustrating. I thought that PFC Jessica Lynch was utterly candid when asked why she joined the Army. She said, "I couldn't get a job, not even in Wal-Mart, in Palestine, West Virginia, and that I joined the Army as a way out." But the point is, these people don't expect to be shot at. They're not going into the armed forces expecting to go into combat. A very large portion of them come from a national minority of one kind or another and suffer considerably by the pressures put on them. And this is one of the things that generate the internal dynamic today. Can the Pentagon of today get enough people into the armed forces to maintain the imperialist policies? One of the things I had in mind in writing this book was that the danger of military populism in the United States would be something like the way the Roman Empire ended with the coming of power of Octavian, and of course his metamorphosis into Augustus Caesar, actually the first military dictatorship. But this reflected the growing size of the standing army, their internal grievances against society and their willingness at some point to turn over power to a dictator who would serve their interests in return for some alleviation of their grievances. That is to say, to put it quite bluntly, I think that it's possible to imagine the defeat of electoral processes in the United States today, given how corrupt they have become. Nonetheless, whoever replaces George Bush, no matter which party or which person, its very hard for me to imagine that person could stand up to the enormous vested interests of the Pentagon, the Military Industrial Complex, and the Intelligence Agencies that have become, because of their secrecy, because of vested interests and economic interests, virtually beyond any democratic oversight.

BONPANE: Well Dr. Johnson, you mentioned one of the characteristics of empire at this time is the matter of 725 bases overseas.

JOHNSON: Let me just say those are 725 that are acknowledged by the Pentagon. There are considerably more that they don't mention, or various odd counting devices. For example, they say one Marine base in Okinawa, when in fact there are ten and they've got them all subsumed under one. None of the bases in England are accounted for at all. They're all disguised as Royal Air Force bases. None of the espionage bases are mentioned. None of the bases in Afghanistan or in Iraq are mentioned, of course. For some odd reason the huge base in Kosovo, Camp Bonsfield, is not mentioned in the latest edition of the Base Status Report.

BONPANE: Now this growth has been going on for over a hundred years. If we look at 1898, we see the beginnings of Guantanamo and also in the Philippines as well. So this has been growing rapidly throughout a century until we arrive at this particular state of having 725, which is the most conservative number, of bases at this time.

JOHNSON: It won't be easily reversed. Its been going on for some time.

BONPANE: Yes, it's very profound. Now the response of the rest of the world seems to be taking place. To me it seems to be in the value of the Euro at this time. Have you noticed this? Is this some type of a protest taking place?

JOHNSON: Well, its almost inevitable that when you have a country that claims to be the "new Rome," that is beyond any rules, doesn't need

245

friends, that lives by its legions, based from Greenland to Australia, that of course, the rest of the world begins to combine against it. They do not do so frontally because they know that they cannot stand up against a direct military contest with the United States. But they begin to do so in a subtle and private, quiet way, just as the world did surrounding the Roman Empire. It's just a process that's much more speeded up. It comes with the speed of FedEx today. I think, of course, there's opposition to the United States in attempts to cut off this exercise of power. The other thing I think that makes a difference is that American imperialism, until the George II administration, was reasonably subtle in that it tried to disguise itself under some abstract concept such as globalization, humanitarian intervention or something of this sort. Globalization was a particularly good one because, spurious as it was, it pretended to reflect ineluctable technological factors that we were just adjusting to. Concretely, it actually meant the attempt by the United States to force its mode of capitalist enterprise on the rest of the world. But with the advent of the ideologists surrounding George Bush in the current administration, we've dropped our pretenses. We now say in so many words that we're out for preventive war against anywhere between 50 and 60 nations, that we don't need the UN, we don't need the International Criminal Court, we don't care about the huge and very huge and very successful edifice of international law that the United States has championed since World War II, so that no one in the future has any doubt about what's coming at them. In many ways, the rest of the world is now concluding that what was wrong with Saddam Hussein is that he *didn't* have nuclear weapons.

BONPANE: I'm speaking today with Dr. Chalmers Johnson, whose book *The Sorrows of Empire: Militarism, Secrecy, and the End of the Republic* will be published on January 13. That's Tuesday. I think the entire world is going to be anxious to see this. Now, one of the characteristics you mentioned in the book, Dr. Johnson, is that there's been no consideration as regards to democracy in the governments where we have placed our bases. You have mentioned Kurdistan, Uzbekistan, and also the brutal leadership that we've imposed on Indonesia, South Vietnam, Taiwan, Cambodia, and the Philippines. This seems to go along with the outreach of the basis, no?

JOHNSON: This has a genuine Roman quality to it. I doubt that there is any more anti-American democracy on earth than Greece and this reflects the imposition on Greece between 1967 and 1974 of the junta of the so-called Greek colonels that was probably as despicable a regime as sponsored by either side throughout the Cold War and the Greeks have not forgotten it. I think any American traveling to the Olympic games this year in Athens ought to give a thought as to what the Greeks think of the Americans. But it's true in South Korea or in any number in any number of places. It's hard to imagine any greater hypocrisy than to have our army kicking in doors in Iraq and uttering simpleminded little phrases about freedom and democracy. We have not been associated with the bringing of freedom and democracy even in places where after the war our government claimed we did such a great job, namely in Japan, which they use as an example of what geniuses we are in implanting democracy in different cultures. It might only make some sense in Japan if you never look at Okinawa, namely the southern most province of Japan, which was under military occupation from 1945 until 1972, and to this day remains essentially a Pentagon colony. It's hard to think of a place where democracy has been more thoroughly and completely smothered by uniformed members of the American military. So I agree with you that it goes on right at the present moment for the new bases that we're establishing right now that Condoleezza Rice and Colin Powell have both said that they take as a model; the string of bases that we've built around the Persian Gulf in really anti-democratic autocracies like Kuwait, Qatar, Oman, the United Arab Republic, Bahrain. These are not places that in any stretch of the imagination are moving toward democracy. Most people in the world identify the United States by the military presence. Americans keep talking about our wonderful popular culture and other such things if you actually concretely lived elsewhere in the world—Latin America, Western Europe, Asia, Africa—the American you're most likely going to see is somebody dressed in a Special Forces uniform.

BONPANE: Well, Dr. Johnson, there's an economic consideration here that each one of these people in these hundreds of bases has to receive a paycheck. Now there is the manufacturing of dollars without production. This seems to me to be one of the reasons a $5000 house costs $500,000 at this time. So many dollars looking for some useful item after all of these people have been paid. But there's been no production in terms of something actually useful. I think there's an economic consideration.

JOHNSON: Its unimaginably expensive. In my last chapter, I try to deliver on what I mean by the "sorrows of empire" and I come up with four sorrows that I describe in such detail. First, perpetual warfare; second, the loss of liberties; third, the disinformation and lying in official communications that seem to govern the people. But the fourth is bankruptcy, and bankruptcy, whatever you think of the effects on our constitutional republic; of the first three, bankruptcy inevitably and instantly creates a crisis and was exactly what you were talking about in looking at the dollar-euro exchange rate, which is now about a $1.25, for a euro that's a very considerable lowering. What this means is that the United States is running fantastic deficits: deficits in our government accounts, in our federal accounts, in our international trade accounts. We are piling up debt in an unbelievable manner, and as Herb Stein, the former chairman of the Council of Economic Advisors, put it, "Things that can't go on forever, don't." That's what we're talking about, it's something that simply can't go on forever. At some point, the people that finance our profligate life-style, above all our expenditures on waste—for instance, our President just signed in November, a $401 billion defense budget that doesn't even include any money even for Iraq, you know, $9 billion for something that won't work and is just corporate welfare for the industrial military complex, namely the ballistic missile defense system (so-called)—that at some point, the rest of the world, the favored of East Asia that send their capital here, will decide that the euro is a better thing to invest in than the dollar, or the American securities market. At that point, we're in extremely serious trouble.

BONPANE: Well, Dr. Johnson, as we compare and contrast Palestine and Iraq, we see a borrowing of Israeli policy in Iraq and oddly enough, we see the same response. We seem to be creating suicide bombers in Iraq. It's absolutely awesome.

JOHNSON: One of the things I try to discuss in my book is that if there is any one thing that I believe, it is that there is really universal agreement among people who have specialized in terrorist incidents over events that are as old as human history, is that one of the strategic intents behind the mind of a terrorist is to illicit from its targeted regime a very damaging military reaction that tends to militarize the situation. And we have played into this more powerfully than you can imagine. Between 1993 and down to 2001 through 9/11, there were five major al-Qaida bombings throughout the world. There have been 17 since then, when Secretary Rumsfeld said the other day, "We need a metric," which is his term, "of how we are doing against terrorism." We have a metric. We're going backwards. And what's happening is that Osama bin Ladin could not obviously be happier with the results that he has achieved on 9/11. He has produced precisely the kind of wrong reaction that you have gotten from the United States, namely, the tendency to use the armed forces in an inappropriate way. They're not prepared to do this. They're not any good at it. They shoot up civilians in Iraq and they create new terrorists. As it stands right now in Iraq, I thought it was absurd when they said we should be better off now that you've captured Saddam Hussein. The truth of the matter is that any young patriotic Iraqi man must now know that with the capture of Saddam Hussein, he can no longer be thought of as a stooge for the old order. He is now just a patriot and until the end of time his moral obligation is to kill Americans.

BONPANE: Dr. Johnson, I know you're very much in touch with Korea, North and South. Now John Lewis, professor emeritus at Stanford University, just had a private delegation to North Korea.

JOHNSON: Very Impressive.

BONPANE: Would you care to comment on that?

JOHNSON: Well, I admire Mr. Lewis' efforts. He is a well-known specialist on attempts between the communist world and ours and recently China, to explore ways of controlling strategy regarding these unimaginably destructive weapons. Well, they're not really weapons, they're forms of state terrorism. But, I admire him for leading a delegation into North Korea and apparently he is having success. This is a way of undercutting the ideological rigidity between the governments, specifically figures like Secretary for Arms Control, John Bolton. The North Koreans refuse to ever see him again because of his insulting remarks to them. I believe Lewis is doing important work in the hope that something will come of it as the North Koreans desperately try to evade what our President has promised them. That is, he has named them as a part of the Axis of Evil, he said he is going to "take them out," he then goes ahead to demonstrate that this is not just wild talk on his part. He goes ahead and attacks unilaterally and contradictory to international law, one of the nations that he so named as the Axis of Evil, Iraq. Under these circumstances, I think that North Koreans have very properly said to themselves, "We're next. We're on the list. The self-proclaimed 'new Rome' is coming after us and the only way you can stop them is with the threat of nuclear weapons." That is, Kim Jung-Il in the

249

North is virtually in the same position as Winston Churchill in 1940 when he said in the face of the Nazi invasion, "If you've got to go, take one with you." He's preparing the basis for taking quite a bit with him if the Americans should attack him. Meanwhile, in that circumstance, he's preparing the fate of Southeast Asia. Southeast Asia is frustrated that now, they're really up against someone who does have weapons of mass destruction, which is causing enormous pressures in countries such as Japan, to prepare themselves to go nuclear. The fear in China of what a nuclear Japan would do to their environment, the fear of the Russians, who are on the border of all of these countries and the tendency to destabilize all of these areas generally. But this can be traced right back to an incompetent policy in the White House and the Pentagon under the current administration.

BONPANE: Well, Dr. Johnson, our U.S. troops, which have been in there for over a half-century seem to make reconciliation with the North more difficult. It doesn't seem to help the situation to have this massive group of some 40,000 troops—

JOHNSON: Thirty-seven thousand. Second Infantry division.

BONPANE: Right, 37,000 troops. That is really awesome. It is not assisting as a catalyst in bringing the two together as apparently the Koreans want to do.

JOHNSON: Well this is a side of militarism, that is the huge vested interest in the army now, the life-style they have now, in 101 American military bases in South Korea. The anti-Americanism in South Korea is just palpable today. The South Koreans were enormously excited by their former president Kim Dae-jung's trip to North Korea in 2000 for which he won the Nobel Peace Prize in attempting to finally reconcile this civil war situation. But without question, the greatest obstacle anyone has in trying to produce peace on the Korean peninsula and to allow the North Koreans, a failed communist regime left over from the Cold War, to allow them some peaceful way to come in from the cold without being overturned and abused by their traditional enemies is American militarism. It is the belief on the part of the United States that nothing should happen in Korea without the purview of our generals and admirals.

BONPANE: I've been speaking today with Dr. Chalmers Johnson, whose book, *The Sorrows of Empire: Militarism, Secrecy, and the End of the Republic*, will be released, Tuesday, January 13th. I hope everybody will have the opportunity to read this very important book. He has previously written the book, *Blowback*, before the attack of 9/11. And now, Dr. Johnson, I just want to thank you for being with us today and we very much appreciate your scholarship and your contribution to our understanding of the fact that we're dealing with the end of the republic, if we don't somehow reverse the trend.

JOHNSON: WELL MY THANKS TO YOU FOR YOUR EFFORTS IN THE SERVICE OF PEACE.

BONPANE: I WANT TO THANK MY ENGINEER, EBEN RAY, AND TO THANK MY PRO-DUCER, LISA SMITHLINE. THIS HAS BEEN WORLD FOCUS. IF YOU'D LIKE A COPY OF THIS PROGRAM, PLEASE GIVE US A CALL AT 323.852.9808.

This is Blase Bonpane.

Blase Bonpane, Ph.D., is director of the Office of the Americas. He served as a Maryknoll Missioner in Guatemala and was expelled from that country in 1967 during a revolutionary conflict. In adition to being a UCLA and California State University professor, contributer to the *Los Angeles Times* and *New York Times*, he is a news commentator and host of the weekly radio program, *World Focus* on Pacifica Radio (KPFK, Los Angeles) and Adelphia Cable TV.

Previous books include: *Guerrillas of Peace on the Air: Radio Commentaries, Reports, and Other Works Which Examine and Promote the Ideology of Peace* (Red Hen Press, 2002) and *Guerrillas of Peace: Liberation Theology and the Central America Revolution* (toExcel Press, "iUniverse.com," 2002).

The Blase Bonpane Collection has been established by the Department of Special Collections at the UCLA Research Library. This is a compilation of both his published and unpublished writings, together with recordings of his lectures and his radio and television programs.

He was named "the most underrated humanist of his decade" by the *Los Angeles Weekly* in 1989.